CARVED WOODEN PILLARS AT SHRI SWAMINARAYAN TEMPLE, AHMEDABAD

(A TESTIMONY TO THE FIRST WAR OF INDIAN INDEPENDENCE)

CARVED WOODEN PILLARS AT SHRI SWAMINARAYAN TEMPLE, AHMEDABAD
(A TESTIMONY TO THE FIRST WAR OF INDIAN INDEPENDENCE)

By
ONKAR CHAUHAN

SHRI SWAMINARAYAN TEMPLE
AHMEDABAD

ABI PRINTS & PUBLISHING CO.
NEW DELHI

CARVED WOODEN PILLARS AT
SHRI SWAMINARAYAN TEMPLE, AHMEDABAD

ISBN-81-86787-09-7

Published in **2003** by

SHRI SWAMINARAYAN TEMPLE
Kalupur, Ahmedabad - 380 001

in association wtih

ABI PRINTS & PUBLISHING CO.
Pooja Apartments, 4B, Ansari Road, Darya Ganj, New Delhi-110 002 (INDIA)
Tel. : 23287589, 23255799; Fax : 91-11-23270385

Printed in India at B.B.N. Printers, New Delhi

This book is dedicated to
Acharyashri
H.H. Tejendraprasadji Maharaj

Yunan-o-Misr Ruma sab mit gaye jahan se
Ab tak magar hai baqi namo-nishan hamara
Kuchh bat hai ki hasti mitati nahi hamari
Sadiyon raha hai dushman daur-i-zaman hamara

Ancient civilisations of Greece, Egypt and Rome have all disappeared from this world
But the elements of our civilisation still continue
Although world-events have been inimical to us for centuries
There is something in our civilisation which has withstood these onslaughts.

CONTENTS

LIST OF ILLUSTRATIONS

17. Pillar No. 8 (Front)
18. Pillar No. 8 (Left)
19. Pillar No. 8 (Right)
20. Pillar No. 9 (Front)
21. Pillar No. 9 (Left)
22. Pillar No. 9 (Right)
23. Pillar No. 10 (Front)
24. Pillar No. 10 (Left)
25. Pillar No. 10 (Right)
26. Pillar No. 11 (Front)
27. Pillar No. 12 (Front)

ACKNOWLEDGEMENT

Working on this monograph has indeed been a very enriching experience.

To begin with, I would first and foremost like to place on record my admiration for late Dr Krishna Deva, a well-known historian and an eminent scholar. His deep understanding of interpretative history of sculptures has encouraged me to delve into the subject. And the result—this monograph—for which I shall remain ever indebted to him.

I am extremely grateful to Dr S.P. Gupta, Secretary; Dr K.N. Dixit, Treasurer; All India Archaeological Society and Dr C. Margabandhu, for providing me an opportunity to present my findings at the All India Archaeological Conference held at Vadodara in November 2001. Subsequently, the paper was also presented at the Indian History Congress, held at Bhopal in the same year.

I immensely benefited by the scholarly suggestions made by Dr Suman Pandye, Banaskata; Dr M.K. Dhavalikar, Deccan College of Pune; Dr V. Shindhe, Pune; Dr A. Sundar, Dharwad; Dr Nayanjyot Lahiri, Delhi University; Dr Rahi, Aligarh University; Dr Lata Akalujakar, Solapur; Dr Malla Mitra, Calcutta; Manavi Sharma, Jaipur and my colleagues Dr B.R. Mani, Shri P.B. Shenger and Shri D.V. Sharma, during the conference at Vadodara. I am also thankful to Dr Suraj Bhan, Kurukshetra; Dr Gunavant Mule, Vedic Mathematician; Dr B.S. Nayik, Mumbai University; Dr Ali, Ujjain University; Dr Avasthi, Allahabad University; Dr G.S. Mane, Amravati University and Dr Mishra, Bhopal, during the Congress.

My special thanks to Dr R.C. Aggrawal, Member Secretary, Indian Council of Historical Research (ICHR), for helping me conclude my work thorough his valuable suggestions.

I am particularly grateful to Dr S.S. Biswas, former Director-General of National Museum, who inspired me to publish this work. My sincere thanks to Shri C.D. Mishra, Shri Sudhir Kumar, Shri V.S. Badigar, but for whom this monograph would not have seen the light of the day.

I deeply appreciate and sincerely thank my wife Sunanda for her unstinted support. Lastly, by the grace and blessings of Acharya Tejendraprasadji, Mahanthswami and Swamins of Swaminarayan temples located at Muli, Dholka, Dholera, Vadtal, Rajkot, Junagadh and Gadada, I have been successful in bringing out this monograph.

C-16, South Motibagh-II,
Nanakpura, New Delhi - 110 021

Onkar Chauhan

A BRIEF HISTORY OF SWAMINARAYAN SECT AND TEMPLE

BHAGAWAN SWAMINARAYAN : INCARNATION OF THE SUPREME LORD ON EARTH FOR RELIGIOUS EMANCIPATION AND SOCIAL SERVICE

The self-realised divine preceptor and reincarnation of Uddhavji, Guru Shri Ramanand Swami, installed his young twenty-one year old celibate disciple Neelkanth Varni as the Head of the Uddhav Sampradaya at Jetpur in Saurashtra on *Ekadashi*, the eleventh day of the bright-half of the month of Kartik, Vikram Samvat 1858, in the year 1802. He was baptised or renamed as Swami Sahajanand and Narayan Muni by his Guru. After assuming *Acharyapad*, Head of the Fellowship, he established Swaminarayan Sampradaya by reconditioning Uddhav Sampradaya. Today it has more than 4,000 grand temples and millions of followers all over the world.

Shri Sahajanand Swami was born in a pious Brahmin family at Chhapaiya near Ayodhya in Uttar Pradesh, on the ninth day of the bright half of the month of Chaitra, Vikram Samvat 1837, i.e. 2 April 1781. His father, Hariprasad Pande, and mother, Shrimati Premavati, ardent devotees of Lord Krishna, are worshipped and adored as Dharmadev and Bhaktidevi respectively in the fellowship. After His parents' demise, He left home at the tender age of eleven to set out on an extensive pilgrimage in search of knowledge and divine experience. He wandered for the next eight years, undergoing severe penance. The wanderings took Him to far-flung places, as He travelled and traversed from the Himalayas to Kanyakumari.

After having widespread religious and philosophical experiences, encounters and discourses; He came to Loj, near the port of the Mangarol in Saurashtra via Pandharpur and Nasik and stayed there with Swami Muktanand, the disciple of Shri Ramanand Swami. Walking long distances in the vast regions of Gujarat, Saurashtra and Kutch, accompanied by a band of pious saints, He awakened a fountain of devotion among the masses. By de-addicting thousands and thousands of people, He put them on the divine track of devotion. He touched the chords of countless men, women and children, old and young, rich and poor, in the fellowship by organising *Samaiya,* the religious congregation for *satsang* or religious fellowship, in the different towns and villages. He accomplished the great work of religious unity by performing *yagnas* and attracted innumerable devotees by celebrating religious festivals at various places. He devoted twenty-eight of his forty-nine years to the cause of religious emancipation and social service and emerged as a great religious and spiritual emancipator in Gujarat, Kutch, Kathiawar, Rajasthan, Maharashtra, Madhya Pradesh and Uttar Pradesh. He awakened the society against religious sham and hypocrisy. His life's mission was so magnificent and divine that during His lifetime, itself people adored and worshipped Him as the incarnation of God by the name Shri Hari, the source of all incarnation, Shri Swaminarayan Bhagwan.

Bhagwan Shri Swaminarayan had pledged three main missions during His incarnation : *(i)* To construct large temples and install idols of the Divine Forms *(ii)* In order to intitiate the seekers of salvation by imparting *mantra deeksha,* spiritual incantation and *Bhagwad deeksha* to the saints. He planned to institute the Seats of Acharyas from *Dharmavansh* to organise and administer the religious order and undertake the responsibility of both the religious and administrative matters and; *(iii)* To create the scriptures of fellowship and to enable the followers to understand religion, knowledge, asceticism (or renunciation) and devotion.

1. The Plan of the Swaminarayan Temple

2. A general view of the Temple

3. A closer look at the Temple

7. Shri Anandanand Muni, who was entrusted the task of building the Temple

8. First Acharyashri H.H. Ayodhyaprasadji Maharaj

9. Present Acharyashri H.H. Tejendraprasadji Maharaj

4. Bhagwan Swaminarayan

5. Shri Radha-Krishna Dev, Swaminarayan Temple

6. Shri Nara-Narayan Dev, Swaminarayan Temple

Once, early in *Brhamamuhurta* on the ninth day in the dark half of the month of Jyestha, Vikram Samvat 1886, Shri Hari woke up and reflected, "Nine magnificent temples installing divine idols of *Nar-Narayan Dev* and other deities have been built. For the refuge and support of the saints and the devotees, we have instituted *Acharyapad,* the seats of Acharyas from *Dharmavansh.* Our missions now are all well accomplished. It is time to return to Our Divine Abode". And soon, winding up all his human activities in this world, He returned to His Divine Abode ... *Akshardham.*

SWAMINARAYAN SAMPRADAYA : SYMBOL OF RELIGOUS AND SECTARIAN INTEGRATION

Shri Sahajanand Swami propagated *Bhagvat Dharma* in a new form at a time when fanaticism, ignorance and anarchy reigned in the religious sphere in India. He integrated and unified the society lost in the labyrinth of religion, sect and factionalism. He imparted a novel approach to the worship and adoration of *panchdev* by installing with reverence, Vishnu, Shiv, Parvati, Ganesha, Sun, Hanumana and other deities in a solemn way. He unified and gathered a cross-section of people under this new *Sampradaya.* No matter whatever their personal deity or the sect in which they had faith, he brought the Hindus, Muslims, Parsis and Christians closer together. He was the pioneer of religious and sectarian integration.

Swaminarayan Sampradaya represents the essence of Hindu *Shastras* which could be easily understood and practised by the common man. It preaches purity in daily life through abhorrence of vices and addictions; promotes tolerance, impartiality and brotherhood; condemns any kind of violence; and believes in equal status for women in the society. Shri Sahajanand Swami's discourses, in simple language, came from his heart and touched every soul. So is the literature of the sect. No religion or sect has a more wide, varied, and distant following. The people, particularly those belonging to the lower strata of the society, continue to join its fold. Swaminarayan Sampradaya thus is the common man's religion which is easy to practise, easier to follow and the easiest to embrace. The religion which is ever fulfilling and ever growing.

In his book entitled *The Capital of Gujarat, Ahmedabad,* Shri Ratnamanirao Bhimrao Jote, observes:

Shri Sahajanand Swami rejected the stratification of the high and the low in *Bhakti* or devotion. His preaching seems to be a wonderful co-ordination of the spirit of service of the Vaishnavas, rigorous self-control of Jainism, *Vishishtadvait,* particular monism of Ramanujacharya, the traditional celebration of the religious festival of Pushtimarg and practical apprehension and understanding of the current situation of the given space and time.

He did not propound any new philosophy but proclaimed his faith in Ramanujacharya's *Vishistadvait* philosophy saying : मतम् विशिष्टाद्वैत में ।

AN EPITOME OF RELIGION AND ARCHITECTURE

Shri Swaminarayan Temple is historically the most important and religiously the most prominent because the main shrine of Nar-Narayan Dev, the first and foremost in the world, was ceremoniously installed by Shri Sahajanad Swami Himself.

His great resolve "to build magnificent temples on earth and install Divine Icons there" was realised through its construction at Ahmedabad.

The then British officer at Ahmedabad, Mr Dunlop, was very impressed by the divine qualities and genius of Shri Hari. He, along with another British officer, Mr Edward, sought special permission all the way from England and gifted a vast piece of land right in the heart of the city of Ahmedabad. The plot of land of Pathakwadi near Navapura in Kalupur was presented with an order inscribing "as long as the sun and the moon shine" on a copperplate. In Vikram Samvat 1857, Shri Hari sent to Ahmedabad the expert of temple construction, Shri Anandanand Muni, accompanied by Govindanand Swami, Gnananand Swami, Ratanji Prasad and others with instructions to make preparations to build a sturdy and magnificent temple with three domes according to the strict principles of the science of architecture there. Shuddhagnanand Swami and some other saints were sent to Dungarpur in Rajasthan for preparation of the holy idols. The temple design and drawings were done by a devotee, an artist named Shri Naranjibhai of Bhuj. The stones for the temple were brought from the quarries at Himmatnagar and Dhrangadhar. Ambaram and Kuber of Visnagar were the principal sculptores.

For the installation ceremony, Shri Hari accompanied by saints, *parshads,* devotees and others arrived at Jetalpur, and then proceeded to camp at the Kankaria Lake on the sixth day of the dark half in the month of Jyestha in Vikram Samvat 1878. Next day, he led a grand procession from Kankaria to Nava Vas via Raipur gate, Manek Chowk and other parts of the city. The citizens had decorated their houses and streets in great grandeur to extend a very warm welcome and had turned out in great numbers on the streets to have a *darshan* of Shri Hari.

Shri Hari was impressed to see the temple and blessed the sculptors and architects and honoured them with turbans, scarfs and gold chains. He also graced the saints and devotees by offering garlands.

The installation ceremony commenced on the first day of the bright half of the month of Phalgun. Thousands of saints and devotees had turned up from all places, far and wide. The function, conducted most ceremoniously as prescribed in the scriptures and performed by 108 brahmins chanting mantras, lasted for three days.

Shriji Maharaj lifted the twin-idols of Shri Nar-Narayan Dev Himself and installed them on the platform of the sanctum sanctorum with *Shodashopachar Pooja,* the sixteenfold rituals prescribed by the Vedas. As recorded in the literature of the Sampradaya, Shriji Maharaj stood in front of the idols for one *muhurt,* i.e. fourty-eight minutes and invested all his powers in the idols. Great light emanated then from His Self and merged with the idols. The installed idols then appeared brighter.

Thereafter, He moved in the sanctum sanctorum and installed the idols of Radha-Krishna to the east of Nar-Narayan Dev and those of Dharma-Bhakti in the west and of Shri Hari Krishan Maharaj Himself. At last He offered coconuts in the sacrificial oblations and the installation *yagna* was concluded.

On this auspicious event, the Britishers gave 101 gun salutes as their homage.

On the fifth day, Shri Hari organised *Choryasi*—a grand feast offered to thousands of brahmins of the city and Daskroi at Kankaria Lake.

Pointing out the significance of Shri Nar-Narayan Dev, Shri Sahajanand Swami had observed:

> The Nar-Narayan Dev, the Lord here, is the Emperor of India and is eternal. Perfect and Supreme Lord Shri Krishna having incarnated in His form on earth, with Dharma Dev and Murti Devi as parents in this world, has been performing penance at Badrikashram for a *Kalpa* (4,320,000,000 years). Hence devotion to Him is graceful for the people of Bharatkhand, India.

In order to establish the unity of His Self and Shri Nar-Narayan Dev, Shri Hari observed:

Shri Nar-Narayan Dev, is in fact Our own form. We have incarnated Ourselves on earth in the human form for *Moksha* or salvation of innumerable *Jivas,* living beings. Let no one see any difference between Shri Nar-Narayan Dev and Us.

Facing north, sturdy and steadfast, octagonal and with a huge dome with three pinnacles, the beautiful temple, is a noble and excellent example of the finest art of both, temple and the woodcarved *haveli* architecture of Gujarat.

ARCHITECTURAL AND ICONOGRAPHIC ELEMENTS OF TEMPLE AND *HAVELI*

Nar-Narayan Dev Temple

The main shrine of Shri Nar-Narayan Dev has two main idols in the form of Shri Govind, sculpted in black stone. They are installed in the holy sanctum, altar hall in the heart of the temple facing north. Both the *chaturbhuj,* i.e. four-armed idols have weapons in the identical order in their upper hands. They hold conch/shells in their lower hands.

Sculpted in the most symmetrical *sambhang* posture, the idols have a proportionate physique, narrow waist, broad shoulders and chest, divine face and adorned headgear; everything is most captivating. Round earrings, wristlets and bracelets, attractive necklaces and rosaries hanging down over the knees and beautiful anklets, are exquisitely engraved as a part of the costumes and ornaments. Sanakadik-snakes and some other deities in miniature size are also installed on both sides of the idols. *Simhasan,* the golden throne, on which the twin idols are enshrined, is an excellent specimen of wooden and metallic art.

In *garbhagriha,* the sanctum sanctorum, on the east of the altar hall the idols of Radha-Krishna Dev on the beautiful, artistic throne are installed a platform. The icon of Krishna is sculpted in black stone and that of Radha in white marble on his left.

Equally fascinating are the *Bhaskarya* style sculptures of winged *Garuda* sitting in the heroic *Veermudra* posture with folded hands; a couple of cows standing, facing each other and a pair of lions. The *Purna-murt* style of sculptures of perfectly chiselled elephant drivers and four *sadhu dwarpals,* sage-sentinals on top of the pillars of the throne and the sun, peacocks, flowers and creepers on the arches sculpted in the *Ardh-murt* style also leave one spellbound.

The pillar of the dome opposite the idols has been graced by Shreeji Maharaj.

On the golden throne on the elevated platform, on the west of *garbhagriha,* the sanctum sanctorum, are installed the idols of Dharma-Bhakti and *dwibhuj,* i.e. two-armed idol of Harikrishna Maharaj in *sambhang,* an upright posture.

This throne, too, is embellished with glorious sculptures of artistic arches, pillars, *Madal*-brackets and *Bhaskarya* style sculptures of saints chanting hymns with musical instruments, cows, elephants, *Garuda* and *Gandharvas,* the celestial singers wearing pretty garlands, are in the background.

The *Sukh-Shaiyya,* blessed bed of the Lord, is also set up in the inner space and there is also a *Panchmukhi Shivalingam.*

A huge *ghumat* or the hemispherical dome, is built on top of the central octagonal pavilion of the temple and smaller hemispherical domes are constructed on the three *pravesh chowkies* or entrances. The Golden Copulas, *Suvarna Kalash,* are mounted on the pinnacle of each of them. This makes the facade of the temple quite fascinating. The *Otta,* platform adjoining the pillar on north of the stairs, has been graced and sanctified by Shreeji Maharaj Himself.

The shrines of Ganesha wearing a scarlet turban in the South Indian style and Hanumana, with a set of teeth as white as pomegranate pips, are installed in *devkulikas* built on both sides of the Shrungar Chowki in the quadrangle. Both the idols are larger than life-size and chiselled according to the tradition of the sect.

The columns and domes of this first temple of the *Sampradaya,* or sect, have been embellished with very artistic *madal-shilp,* sculptures of dancers in a wide range and variety of postures. The damsels with musical instruments radiate and exude emotions.

These dancers are endowed with symmetrical and proportionate physique. Their artistic postures with beautiful limbs, costumes and ornaments representing local and regional cultural tradition have been painted in most wonderful colours revealing the modern technique.

Quite an artistic parapet is constructed around the columns and slabs of the temple all over. The corners of balconies have been decorated with the artistically carved figures of tigers.

Since all the three *garbhagrihas,* sanctum sanctorums of Shri Swaminarayan Temple are in a row, its three domes are also in one line. These domes are constructed in rectilinear Chalukya or Nagara style of architecture. Shrungar Chowki is also the passage or *pravesh chowki,* the entrance of the temple. The staircase of the temple is quite simple; by climbing up one can reach the entrance. The columns of the temple are of variegated shapes and on the encircling outer pillars there are captivating *madal-shilps*—sculptures in the brackets, of dancing damsels in a variety of postures. There are decorative and semicircular *Toran* arches over the pillars of all the three entrances in *Gavaluka* style.

Akshar Bhuvan : The Museum of Graced Objects

The three-storeyed new building known as Akshar Bhuvan stands on the south-eastern side of the main structure. The idol of Bal Ghanshyam, evocative of profound emotions in white marble, is installed in the ground floor. Objects sanctified and graced by Shreeji Maharaj have been exhibited on the ground and the first floor. On southern side there is an inn for the pilgrims.

Haveli in the East

This is a two-storeyed *haveli* or mansion. On the pillars of the portico on the ground floor are engraved the captivating sculptures of animal heads, flowers and creepers which are superb specimens of the art of woodcarving. There are stores and treasures of Nar-Narayan Dev on the ground floor. The Sanskrit *pathshala* and music school are located on the first and the second floors. The residence, kitchen and the dining hall for *brahmcharis*, the celibate students, are located in the backyard. The well of the inn of *brahmacharis* and the *chhatri*, the domed shade, where Shri Hari used to take bath, are places graced by Him. The first and second floors are used as residence for the saints.

Rang Mahal : The Temple of Mota Ghanshyam Maharaj

In the north-east at the rear of the *haveli* there is a way leading to the temple of Mota Ghanshyam Maharaj, known as Rang Mahal. Shri Hari used to live here on his visits to Ahmedabad.

A beautiful, pleasant and lively life-size idol of Shreeji Maharaj, carved in wood in standing *sambhang* position, bestowing blessings with His graceful hands, was installed here fifty years after the construction of the temple. Not only within the sect but also outside it, it is one of the finest and glorious specimens of art of wood sculpture in Gujarat.

The Main *Haveli* in North : The Three–Storeyed Mansion

This *haveli* was constructed by H.H. Acharya Shri Keshavprasadji Maharaj in 1871.

The structure of this *haveli* with three storeys rest, on the octagonal and square wooden pillars. The *Ardh-murt* relief sculptures of flowers and creepers engraved on them are quite fascinating.

Equally rich, in the art of woodcarving in free-hand design on the shapely *Bharani*, are the angles of the pillars on which rest balconies or porches and so the projected structures, *tandika, falna,* etc.

Sabhamandap, an extensive Central Hall or the congregation place (134 x 45 sq. ft.), has been constructed on the ground on sixty pillars. There are giant size *madal-shilp* sculptures on twelve high pillars in the front row on which rests the portico of the first floor, capture our attention with its great artistic appeal. The beautiful sculptures of flying Hanumana lifting the Devgiri Mountain in his palm and with his mouth open, showing his teeth, and of potbellied Ganesha, wearing a scarlet turban in the South Indian style, as well as miniature sculptures of several soldiers armed and dressed in Marathi turbans and costumes and herds of monkeys have been created in the religious tradition in the wooden sculptures. All this manifests the finest and noblest examples of Gujarati art in wood.

It is believed that the history of 1857 revolt in India, depicting the Rani of Jhansi and other heroes is narrated in the carvings of these pillars.

Beside these artefacts, sculptures of lions and elephants, birds like peacocks and parrots and perfectly engraved leaves and flowers decorate the panels. The beams, ceilings, and lower sections are beautified by a wide range of engravings and artistic sculptures and free-hand designs.

In this mansion, Acharya Maharajshri sits on the wooden seat of Shri Hari in the Congregation Hall.

On one of the two *Ottas* or platforms in the Assembly Hall, Shri Hari used to serve food to the saints and sit on a chair.

The new residence for the saints, Vrajendraprasad Mahal and the dining hall for the devotees are also situated here.

Charanarvind or the Footprints and Chhatri

In the courtyard, right in front of the northern entrance of the temple, the replicas of Shri Hari's Footprints with their auspicious signs and symbols are installed under a *chhatri* or domed seat. This *chhatri* is in white marble with its columns in Victorian style of architecture and decorated with the sculptures of female musicians, is an excellent example of art.

It is the same *chhatri* where Shri Hari had played with colours during the festival of Holi.

Haveli in the West

The four-storeyed *haveli*, the mansion, in the western side of the main *chowk* is a superb specimen of woodcarved *haveli* architecture and *Vastu* planning in Gujarat. Acharya Maharajshri Vasudevprasadji's seat is located on the first floor, a large assembly hall is on the second floor, and there are various rooms on the top floor.

Since this mansion was constructed as the residence of Acharya Maharajshri, it has more facilities and is decorated with chandeliers, suspended lamps and large mirrors. The brackets of the pillars of the portico and the arches in the ground floor and those of the lobbies of the first, second and third floors have been adorned with carvings in geometrical designs and a variety of flower and creeper motifs.

The columns and stone bases are artistically embellished by engravings.

Baio-ni-Haveli : Temple for Ladies

One can go to the Ladies' *haveli*, Mansion for Women, passing through an ornamental gate of the western mansion, the residence of the ascetic and dedicated ladies of the sect. In one of the rooms on the ground floor, there is a full-size wooden idol of Ghyanshyam Maharaj.

Only those dedicated ladies who have renounced, and who can worship and perform religious rites and rituals, live here. Since this *Haveli* is exclusively meant for the women, there is obviously no admission for men. This is one of the finest architectural creations replete with excellent wooden engravings, the like of which are rarely found elsewhere in Gujarat.

Formely, this *Haveli* was occupied by the family of Maharajshri.

Old *Chhatri* : Assembly Ground under the Neem Tree

Shri Hari used to sit here under the *Neem* tree and address the congregation in the temple of Shri Nar-Narayan Dev.

The Gateway

The Central Gateway of the temple is artistic and magnificent, manifesting the triple confluence of local, regional and British styles of architecture and sculpture at their best.

A variety of sculptures on the Gateway reveal the adjoining Marathi and Rajasthani folk cultures and costumes. The engravings on the columns with vertical lining are in corinthian style whereas the coverings of the projected pavilions remind us of the Mughal architecture. The statues of the women wearing frilled blouses and petticoats and carrying kids on their waists depict the Gujarati woman.

A pair of courageous Kathi youths facing a tiger with swords, wearing turbans, half jackets, *dhotis* and waist-girdles and costumes are engraved on the arch of the gate. The relief works presenting the doorkeepers in Kathiawari costumes are also excellent examples of the contemporary sculptures of the time. Equally attractive are the two pairs of wrestlers and hunters with guns in relief work.

GREAT TRADITION AND ACHARYAS FROM DHARMKUL

The lineage of Shriji Maharaj is Dharmkul. Shriji Maharaj graced the highest seat of the supreme preceptor of Shri Swaminarayan Sampradaya on 16 November 1801, when Ramanand Swami installed him by conducting a majestic celebration at Jetpur in the Saurashtra region. Shriji Maharaj strengthened the faith of the followers and the saints and spread this axiomatic sect in the region of Saurashtra, Kutch and Gujarat which then spread to all the provinces of India. He wielded majestic and divine powers and conducted sessions of instant meditational trance; exhibited divine episodes, conducted *yagnas* in accordance with Vedic scriptures, built a majestic retinue of thousands of saints wielding divine power inclusive of released souls of Akshardham; brought the atheists and irreligious people back into the fold of axiomatic religion; changed the heart of criminals, cheaters, looters and sanctified them by raising devotional love in their heart. He constructed a society wedded to the Vaishnava path of pure devotion. He banished vices like addiction, theft, atrocities on women, killing the female child, black magic, meditation of evil spirits, etc. Jivan Mukta saints wrote thousands of devotional songs and created immortal literature and great religious scriptures in Sanskrit, Gujarati and Braj language. They paid visits to every place – towns, villages and colonies, fields and farms – to preach Satsang. He constructed great temples to strengthen faith in God. Shri

Hari himself formulated a constitution of the sect and dictated it personally as Desh Vibhag. Through this constitution, he formed a preceptor (Acharya) for each Desh. He adopted the sons of his elder and younger brother from the Dharmkul and installed them as Acharya on each seat and himself did the *Gaddi Abhishekam.*

ADI ACHARYA AYODHYAPRASADJI MAHARAJ (1826–1868)

Ayodhyaprasadji Maharaj, the son of the elder brother of Lord Shriji Maharaj, became the first Acharya of Lord Narnarayandev desh at the age of seventeen when Lord Shriji Maharaj adopted him as his son and installed him on the highest seat of supreme preceptor on 20 November 1826. *Gaddi Abhishekam* of the first Acharya Ayodhyaprasadji was carried out personally by Shriji Maharaj.

Ayodhyaprasadji though he was a scholar and spiritually wise, had always been humble, polite and caring. Though possessing divine majesty, he lived an ego-free life. Simplicity and humbleness were the core of his nature. Great and famous people touched his feet, but he never had the slightest trace of ego. He travelled far and large, covering Kutch and the other border districts of Gujarat to spread Satsang. He constructed Maha Mandirs at Ḍungarpur, Idar, Jetalpur, Siddhapur, Mandavi and Chhapaiya and installed idols of Gods with majestic celebrations. He founded at Ahmedabad, the first Universal Institute of the Sampradaya to teach Sanskrit language, grammar, literature and religious scriptures to the saints and Satsangis of both the dioceses. This institute – Sanskrit Pathshala – has grown today into a great seat of learning and imparting Sanskrit education at school, college and research level, with a well-stocked library of rare books and research periodicals. Ayodhyaprasadji Maharaj guided and lead this Sampradaya by holding the seat of Acharya for forty-two years.

SHRI KESHAVPRASADJI MAHARAJ (1868–1890)

Shri Keshavprasadji Maharaj, the second descendant heir of Shri Hari and the son of Ayodhyaprasadji Maharaj, held the highest seat of the supreme preceptor of Shri Narnarayandev diocese from 18 February 1868 onwards at the age of thirty-six and lead the Sampradaya for years by promoting scriptural knowledge, creation of Satsang literature and full support to the scholars. He never accepted any personal gift from the followers. He submitted all such gifts to Lord Narnarayandev sitting at the diocese headquarters – Shri Swaminarayan Temple, Kalupur Ahmedabad. Analytical study of the scripture was the core of his nature. He had arranged for preparing the treatise on Satsangi Bhushan written in Sanskrit. He himself wrote a treatise named *Anvaydeepika* on "Hari Vakya Sudha Sindhu". Literary creation and publication attained its summit during the reign of this Acharya. He established Satsang in the princely states of Kutch and Saurashtra and constructed temples at Karachi, Prantij, Mansa, Dabhan, Charadava, and Visnagar.

SHRI PURUSHOTTAMPRASADJI MAHARAJ
(1890–1901)

Acharya Purushottamprasadji Maharaj, the son of Keshavprasadji Maharaj, became the Acharya on 9 April 1890 as the third descendant heir of Shriji Maharaj. He was sociable, loving and caring by nature but was also hot tempered and occasionally furious if he found anybody slighting the sect, saints or Satsangis. He used to organise splendid sabhas and festivals in the big cities to exhibit the majesty and glory of the sect. He conducted religious tours from village to village with a huge retinue, camping equipment and Satsangi volunteers, befitting a great religious head. He constructed a study and research based treatise on *Vachanamrit* to help aspirants of ultimate truth. He arranged scholarly research of *Vachanamrit* and published it in a gorgeous form beffiting a religious scripture. The majestic and artful gate of Ahmedabad Temple and restructured Narayanghat are his blissful gifts to the Satsang.

SHRI VASUDEVPRASADJI MAHARAJ
(1901–1937)

Shri Vasudevprasadji Maharaj being the fourth descendant heir of Dharmkul and Shri Hari, held this seat at an early age of three years. He was a scholar of Sanskrit and Prakrit scriptures and exhibited excellent fluency in Sanskrit and English language. He installed idols of God in Vali (Rajasthan), Ayodhya (Uttar Pradesh) and Bamroli (Madhya Pradesh) by constructing temples. Centenary year of Lord Shriji Maharaj's elemental departure from the earth was celebrated by him on a large scale in accordance to Vedic rituals. Centenary year of Shikshapatri was celebrated by him amidst great devotional fervour and a majestic seminar was organised on that occasion to suitably honour the Vaishanava Acharyas, Shankaracharyas, Mandaleshwaras and scholars from all over India.

SHRI DEVENDRAPRASADJI MAHARAJ (1937–1969)

Acharya Devendraprasadji Maharaj the fifth descendant heir of Shri Hari became the supreme preceptor of this sect at the tender age of fifteen years in 1937. Devendraprasadji possessed supreme virtues of tranquility and patience besides profound spiritual wisdom and scholarship. This Dharm Vanshi head, instilled great spiritual force in the Sampradaya and spread it world-wide. He organised splendid centenary festivals of installation ceremony of Gods in the temples at Chhapaiya, Mandavi and Siddhapur, and constructed Narnarayan Building, Ghanshyam Building, Asarwa Swaminarayan Bagh and the educational complex of Ambavadi-Ellisbridge to accomodate visiting Satsangis, Gurukul students, higher educational institutions, etc. He gave great impetus to the publication of religious literature, founded a publication division within the diocese campus at Shri Swaminarayan Temple, Kalupur and published Satsangi Bhushan, Satsangi Jivan and Harikrishna Lilamrit, etc., scriptures with Gujarati translation. Satsang literature attained climax in publicity and its reach. Twenty thousand copies of *Vachanamrit* were distributed during his period, besides print-form of other scriptures and discourses. Twenty-five thousand copies of complete works of each Nand Sant were distributed. Sanskrit-Pathshala was transformed into a centre of Sanskrit learning and research.

H.H. ACHARYA 1008 SHRI TEJENDRAPRASADJI MAHARAJ IN OFFICE SINCE 1969

H.H. Acharya Maharaj Shri Tejendraprasadji is holding this highest seat of supreme preceptor (Acharya) of the diocese since 1969. He is the elder son of late (Acharya) Shri Devendraprasadji Maharaj and had taken reins of the diocese in his hand at the age of twenty-five years as the sixth descendant heir of Dharm Vansh and Shri Hari. He is a well-read scholar and wields absolute hold over English, Hindi, Gujarati and Sanskrit. He has studied in depth the literature and scriptures. He founded the International Swaminarayan Satsang Organisation to facilitate the Satsang activities of millions of Satsangi families residing in farflung continents and countries, and are engaged in business, professional and industrial activities. He has constructed more than one hundred full-fledged temples besides a large number of Harimandirs for Satsang in overseas nations. Satsang activities are being conducted regularly at all these places through the highest seat of Lord Narnarayandev at Ahmedabad Temple. During his Satsang services as Lalji Maharaj, he had headed the Acharya Devendraprasadji Kelavani Trust as Managing Trustee and had developed it into a centre of higher learning and research providing learning experiences right from nursery to university, with ancillaries like boarding, lodging and free education. He founded the Shri Swaminarayan periodical in 1968, which is now being published simultanously in English, Hindi and Gujarati. His religious tours, spread throughout India and the world and covering hundred or more overseas nations and states, strengthens the faith of the Satsangis and instills spiritual force to Satsang activities and social services. His presence is blissful, his words are enlightening.

FUTURE ACHARYA AND H.H. LALJI MAHARAJ 108 SHRI KOSHALENDRAPRASADJI MAHARAJ

H.H. Lalji Maharaj 108 Shri Koshalendraprasadji Maharaj is the future Acharya of Shri Narnarayandevdesh diocese. He is strengthening the faith by conducting youth Satsang camps in India and abroad. These whole time camps are tailor made, befitting the needs of the particular location and the resident youth of that area and are executed accordingly in full-time schedule of one day, three days or a week-long camping with practical training, spiritual discourses, debating on subtle topics of Satsang, lodging and boarding. Besides such Satsang and religious activities, camps are being organised by him to provide medical and health services to the Satsangis and common people to strengthen relations between Satsang and Satsangis and also between devotees and devotion. The coverage of Satsang is rapidly increasing by employing various means like publications, periodicals, audio, video and television serials. All these are being distributed, transmitted and shown throughout the continents and nations under his direct supervision.

Shastri Nirgundasji
Mahant Swami
Shri Swaminarayan Mandir,
Kalupur, Ahmedabad-1.

INTRODUCTION

Instinct, impulse and emotion encourages man to mould his surroundings according to his dreams, desires and creativity. So intense has been his involvement with nature, that it left him awestruck. The breathtaking scenic beauty created at sunrise and sunset, the drifting clouds in the sky, all made man an ardent lover of nature.

Drawing inspiration from nature, man got sensitised to the movements and actions around him, like, the trotting of animals and flying of birds. The result, he began recording his observations in all available forms, that existed in those days. Such records which treasure man's creativity of the bygone eras are available even today in the form of prehistoric cave paintings, or rock-shelter art. The major subjects dealt with in these cave paintings are animals, war scenes, dances, sexual poses, nudes and other day-to-day events. These are living examples of his creativity. India, China, South Africa, France and many other countries are full of such evidences.

Gradually, as man progressed from being a food gatherer to a food producer, several new dimensions towards his love for nature emerged. After the initiation of script and symbols, man ascribed different but befitting meanings to various events. Thus, language came into existence. Though language at the beginning was confined to special creed, race or tribe, it spread, keeping pace with man's progress. Rise of trade and commerce resulted in the growth and development of language. The interaction of groups and tribes led to the formation of different societies and kingdoms which further strengthened the stability and evolution of many languages and scripts. The origin and development of languages offered a new platform to man to express himself through the medium of words and literature. These were the direct results of man's creative instincts. Consequently, he was able to give expression to his creativity through painting and literature. The various shades of leaves and butterflies he saw, led him to add colour to his imagination and reach the zenith of art and creativity.

Man's sensitivity, understanding of the surroundings and new developments added greater clarity to his creative expressions. His observation of the dancing peacock, the rhythmic movement of the snake's hood, the merrymaking of the deer over the head of a *Gajavyala* and the majestic gait of the elephant, compelled him to imbibe these movements and actions. Thus evolved a new medium of creativity—dance.

Slowly, his appreciation of sound began to develop. The music created by the whistling wind of the forest and the eerie silence of the night left him mesmerised. Through experience he realised that variation in music could be generated if air is let out through controlled medium. This led to the invention of seven basic musical notes. The permutation/combination of these notes taught him to create music and invent musical instruments. Soon, he stepped into the world of music with new knowledge of sounds and songs. Various notes of music and songs were invented and developed by him with the progress of his economy within the parameters of time and space.

Along with dance and music, man acquired the art of sculpture. This was facilitated by the ample and easy availability of mud, stone and wood. In addition, the size and shape of various animals and birds, the facial expression and body language of humans encouraged him to incorporate these peculiarities in the sculptures.

The development of painting, literature, music, dance, sculpture, may belong to different groups, castes, creeds, race, kingdom or nation that may totally differ from each other but the thought behind these has remained the same and they have a universal application. Today, we can study each of man's expressions by differentiating them on the basis of style, colour, plasticity and by various other ways suitable to our aim. However, we cannot differentiate art from its basic formation, which is based on practical experiences, imaginations and ingenuity of the artists.

The art of story-telling, is the soul of Indian sculpture and paintings. The prehistoric, ancient and medieval India has numerous examples of these art forms. The famous rock-shelters of Bhimbetka in Madhya Pradesh and Mirzapur in Uttar Pradesh are examples of story-telling through rock paintings by prehistoric man. All the subjects which had a bearing on man have been rightly placed as scenes of story-telling through forms of line paintings. The famous Ajanta and Bagh caves are the finest examples of story-telling in India. The Buddhist *Jataka* stories have been picturesquely depicted in these caves. This work may not be contemporary to the life of the Lord but probably a few centuries later than the actual happening of these incidents. In the Ajanta cave paintings, we find direct and symbolic expressions pertaining to the dreams and other events associated with Buddha's life. These are befitting examples of story-telling through colour.

Similarly, the sculptures of Mathura and Gandhara art are full of examples of story-telling. The Amravati, Bharhut, Sanchi and other stupas of Buddhist era have many panels depicting *Jataka* stories. The Bharhut stupa has scenes from Manha, Nandi-Vishala, Vrsabha, Bharhut, Chaddanta, Bharhut and Ajanta caves 10 and 17, Guthapana, Hasti, Kakkata, Latukika, Matiposaka, Bhojajaniya, Mahakapi, Nigrodhamiga, Tipallathamiga, Kuru, Nacaha, Kutkkuta, Cakkavaka Hamsa *Jataka* at cave no. 17 at Ajanta, Kapota, Sammodamana, Bhisa, Aranna, Dubhiyamakkata, Mannikantha, Aramadusaka, Litta, Gahapatai, Uraga, Alambusa, Ambacora, Indasamanagotta, Mahabodhi, Sarabhanga, Sangamvacara, Timingala, Krudhamma, Kusa, Mahajanika, Mugapakha, Makhadava, Sonaka, Takkariya, Asadisa, Asilakkhana, Dabhapuppha, Cammastake, Vannupatha, Viseyha, Vidurapandita, Mahaumagga, Suci. Mulapriya *Jataka* have found mention in different stone sculptures.

The Chaddanta *Jataka,* Hasti *Jataka,* Hamsa *Jataka,* Mahajanaka *Jataka,* Syama *Jataka,* Vasanttara *Jataka,* Vidurapandita *Jataka,* Mahaumagga *Jataka* are painted in caves nos. 10, 15, 16 and 17 in Ajanta.

The Burmese *Jataka* stories like Neru, Palasa, Uluka, Baveru, Sibi, Vattaka, Canda Kinnara, Samugga, Migapotaka, Dasabrahmana, Manikantha, Mudalakkhana, Tiriavaccha, Samudavanaja, Kundakasindhava, Tittira, Kayasindha, Uraja, Amba, Avarya, Mittaniitta, Matanga, Matarodana, Takka, Upadanadusaka, Komayaputta, Valahassa, Kanhadipayana, Kaccapa, Kimacanda, Davadhamma, Gandhara, Gangamala, Kalinga, Kanvera, Kamanita, Kumbha, Mandhatu, Makhadava, Nanacchanda, Sadhina, Srikalakanni, Srikaladanni, Sucaca, Sumedhapandita, Udaya *Jataka*, Ayacilabhata, Bhikhu, Parampart, Dightikasala, Dutyapalayi, Ekaraja, Godha, Rajovada, Tithi, Tilamutthi, Aykuta, Dubhalakattha, Vannaroha, Ahigundika, Catudevera, Manisa, Sambhava, Somdatta, Kamatappatu, Satapatta, Thusa, Khadirangara and Radha have been sculptured in stone.

Even the Davadhamima *Jatakas* of Siam (Thailand) and the Vasanttara *Jataka* of Nepal, figure in Indian sculptures.

All the *Jatakas* mentioned have been collated, recorded and scripted in the Buddhist books, by the scholars. The Buddhist chronicles reported from India, Burma, Siam, China, Ceylon, Pakistan and Afghanistan need not be found to be in Pali. Sanskrit, Burmese, Chinese, Simhalese, Siamese, are also used to describe these stories. The study of these *Jataka* stories reveals that all these are not related to the reincarnation of Buddha. At present, we know 550 *Jataka* stories from various sources. The study of these reveals that many of the stories are not related to the reincarnation, teaching and preaching of the Lord. Some of the *Jataka* stories are also related to the ethical, moral and social conditions of the society and the state. Reference has been made to evils like adultery, extortion, atrocities upon women and depiction of prevailing corruption in the society in these stories. A visual depiction of these is seen in the sculptured works of those days. A suitable example cited below conveys the authenticity of the above statement.

The story of a Yuva Majhakiya *Jataka* has not been mentioned in the list of Ceylon Buddhist stories, nor has the story been identified by Subhuti. Dr Alexander Cunningham recognised it on the basis of striking representation of the legend of Upakosa, the young wife of Vararuchi as told in the *Brihatkatha* of Kshemendra and in the

Kathasaritasagara of Somadeva. Subhuti suggests that Majhakiya is the name of a country which is likely enough but has not been of any assistance in identifying the Bharhut sculpture with anyone of the Pali *Jataka* of Ceylon. Perhaps, the title simply means the 'young woman *Jataka*'.

Dr Cunningham erred in identifying these *Jataka* stories because of his background. Several languages spoken in India have got a word *Majhakiya* which literally means one who creates humour or mockery. There is no name of any nation or kingdom as *Majhakiya* as stated by him. Though, the semblance of the story sculptured in stone at Bharhut with *Brihatkatha* and *Kathasaritasagara* needs no more clarification when we go through the details described below.

"The Story of Upakosa" as told by Kshemendra in the *Brihatkatha* has been translated by Dr Buhler and as it would be diluted by curtailment, I quote it at full length. On comparing the sculpture with the story, the principal figure can be recognised at once. In the midst is King Nanda seated on the throne and to the right is the young wife Upakosa, pointing to the four baskets, in the foreground containing her four lovers. Three of the baskets have been opened, thus exposing the lovers' faces while the fourth has just arrived on the shoulders of two porters. I wish to draw particular attention to the baskets as the word used by Kshemendra is *manjusha,* meaning a basket and not a box.

FROM THE *BRIHATKATHA*

Having heard this (story of the origin of Pataliputra) and having received all sciences from my teacher, I (Vararuchi) who dwelt at my ease, obtained in marriage the daughter of Guru Upavarsha called Upakosha. After I married Upakosha whose eyes resembled blue lotuses, I became the owner of the empire over which Cupid and vassal of all happiness rules. Whilst I, living in the company of Vyadi and Indradatta, acquired the fame of omniscience, a pupil of Varslia, Panini by name, who was formerly a blockhead, obtained by virtue of his austerities, keeping his sense in subjection a new grammar from Siva. Disputing with me for eight days, he proved himself an opponent of equal force. When I conquered him at the end of that period, Hara bewildering me by growl, bereft me, through anger, of the recollection of Indra's grammar. After I had suddenly forgotten that work, I resolved to perform austerities in order to obtain the sight of Bharga, who is the destroyer of cupid and the wish-fulfilling husband of Parvati. I placed money for the household expenses in the hands of a neighbour, a Vaniya called Hiranyagupta. After I was gone, my faithful Upakosha, though left alone in the beauty of her fresh youth, being versed in the Vedas, performed the vow which is becoming for wives whose husbands are absent. Time passed on and once a young *faujdar* of the king, a domestic priest and a minister saw that beauty. With the swanlike gait, who bathed daily and played with the thick spray, wore a thin and transparent garment, whose broad hips resembled sandbanks, who had a dark blue complexion, whose eyes had the appearance of newly-opened lotuses and who was bud of Cupid, walking like Yamuna to the Ganges. Gazing at her, all three fell in love. First amongst them, the minister said to her, "Love me". She who had finished bathing, seeing that night had gone, became afraid and spoke to him, "Be it so, on the third day at mid-fall, I will meet you secretly". Speaking thus to him she went. After leaving him she addressed the domestic priest to this effect, "On the third day hence, in the second watch of the night I shall be at your disposal". Turning away from him she said to the *faujdar*, "On the third day hence, in the third watch of the night I will be ready to do whatever you say". After she had made this assignation, they let her go and she went home, filling as it were, by her frightened glances the sky with lotuses.

Being in want of her husband's money she tried to remedy its concealment (by the banker). But Hiranyagupta asked her for an assignation in her house. She said to him, "On the third day hence, at the end of the night I will obey thee, what harm is here (in my doing it?)". She told that story to her domestics. When the third day had come, the excellent minister, trembling and having lost all control over himself, entered her house at night , where the lamps had been extinguished. Upakosha called him by his name and said, "On you I have placed my affection". At her order he entered a dark room in the interior of the house.

There the maidservant smeared for a long time the limbs of the lover with the soft unguent consisting of oil lamp soot. But when in the second watch of the night the domestic priest came in haste, Upakosha showed (to the first lover) an open wooden box and said, "Enter quickly, here comes the master of the house" and made him enter it. Closing it with an iron bolt, she said to the domestic priest, "You must not touch me without having bath". He also was treated in the same manner (as the first lover). When he had been anointed with oil and soot, the third also came. Forsooth, who escapes being deceived and made a fool of by the rogue cupid. After the priest, overwhelmed with fear, had been disposed of in the same box (as the first lover), the third also, in his turn, was made to resemble a goblin. At the end of the night the excellent Vaniya, Hiranyagupta arrived. The *faujdar* was concealed likewise in the wooden box. Then Upakosha facing the box spoke to the Vaniya, "Give me the deposit". Hiranyagupta replied, "Love me, sweet smiling one. I have the money, fair-browed one, which your husband deposited with me". Hearing this she exclaimed in a loud voice, "Hear ye deities of the house, be witnesses ye goblins, he has my property". Speaking thus she defaced him also with lamp soot. Then she said, "The night has passed, go". Quickly the Vaniya went forth covering his face from fear of the people. Wise Upakosha who had thus protected her virtue, after his departure, started early for the audience hall of King Nanda. The king was informed that the daughter of Upavarsha, the faithful wife of Vararuchi had come and he honoured her there. She said, "O king, the Vaniya Hiranyagupta conceals great wealth which my husband deposited with him. It is now for you, Lord, to give orders". After that, when that liar had been summoned, Upakosha said, "Lord, at home I have witnesses, order my household gods to be brought who are kept in a box; they will declare the truth". The wooden box was brought at the king's command and placed by the bearers in the midst of the assembly. Then the faithful wife spoke again, "He ye deities, who are worthy of constant worship, tell the truth for my sake. If you remain silent in this matter of evidence, I shall quickly burn the box". Hearing this, they said, full of fear, "Forsooth thy property is in the hands of Hiranyagupta. We three are witnesses to that". All present in the assembly who heard this miraculous answer were astonished. They opened the box and saw the naked men smeared with soot. When the king had been informed of the circumstances of the case, he punished them by fine and honoured Upakosha as his spiritual sister.

The version of the legend given by Somadeva in the *Kathasaritasagara* is almost the same as that of Kshemendra except that during the absence of her husband, Upakosha became the object of the addresses of the king's banker, family priest, the commander of the guards and the princes' tutor. However, Upakosha outsmarted them and had them summoned before King Nanda and the court. Presenting a petition to the king, Upakosha stated that the banker sought to appropriate property entrusted to him by her husband Vararuchi. Thus, Upakosha had the culprits banished as criminals and earned the admiration of the entire city.

A much more modern version of the same legend is found in the *Bahar-Danish*, in the story of the merchant Hassan and Gauhar, the daughter of a *parsa* or devotee. The following is an abridgment of the legend:-

A merchant named Hassan, when out hunting and met a very beautiful girl. The two at once fell in love. As she was the daughter of a devotee, Hassan was in despair, but by her instructions he became an assiduous attendant at prayers and so managed to obtain the consent of others to their marriage. Shortly afterwards Hassan became poor and his wife Gauhar or the 'Pearl' embroidered a piece of cloth which he took to the bazaar for sale. When the kotwal saw this fine piece of embroidery, he accused the merchant of having stolen it. On hearing that Hassan's wife was very beautiful, he seized her also and sent them both to the wazir, who put them in prison. At night, they were released by the kotwal's servant who had fallen in love with Gauhar.

After various adventures they settled in another city where Hassan was soon imprisoned on a false accusation. She at once went to the kotwal to demand justice, but the kotwal fell in love with her and said that her husband could only be released if she acceded to his wishes. Feigning consent, she pointed out her house to him and fixed that very night for his visit. She then went to the court of the qazi to complain of the kotwal's conduct; who was no better than the kotwal. For, the qazi having also fallen in love with her would only agree to release her husband on the same terms as proposed by the kotwal. She again feigned consent and fixed that night for his visit, but a little later than the time appointed for the kotwal.

On her way home, Gauhar bought two bottles of wine for the entertainment of her guests. When the kotwal arrived, she proposed that as the whole night was before them for enjoyment he had better begin the evening with wine. So the kotwal drank and became slightly drunk. Then there was a cry that the qazi was coming and the kotwal being frightened, begged Gauhar to hide him. Unfortunately, there was no accessible place for concealment, except a large earthen vessel, which was securely fastened by Gauhar.

The qazi then came in and was treated to wine in the same way as the kotwal, when he heard a loud knocking at the door and a cry

"The wazir is coming". Frightened, he begged the lady to conceal him somewhere so she put him in a large gunny bag and fastened its mouth.

Gauhar then went to sleep and in the morning hired coolies to carry the earthen vessel and the sack and took them before the king, from whom she demanded justice. The vessel and the sack were opened, the kotwal and the qazi were dragged out and sentenced to be beheaded. Merchant Hassan was released from the prison and returned home to his faithful wife, the 'Pearl'.

A similar story still prevalent amongst the people of other places, is the legend of Dinajpur titled the "Touchstone", of which only the later part need be narrated. As the kotwal was going round the city, he saw the girl on the roof of a house and said to the garland-maker, "I will come and see your sister tonight". He replied, "My sister has made a vow that no one shall come and visit her unless he presents her with a touchstone". The kotwal promised it and went away. After this, the king's councillor saw the girl and said to the garland-maker, "I will come and visit you tonight". By the girl's order the garland-maker agreed and told the councillor to come at the first watch of the night. After this the prime minister came and having made an arrangement that he should come at the second watch in the night, he went away. Thereafter, the king who had came out to enjoy the air saw the girl on the roof and said that he would come at the last watch of the night. When the girl heard that they were all coming, she took a large pot, mixed in it two seers of milk and one seer of water and put it on the fire. When it was evening she placed a stool near the fire for herself and another stool for the others to sit on and proceeded to mix the milk and water. In the meantime, the kotwal came bringing the touchstone with him; so the girl took it and invited him to drink the milk and water, which she prepared and they talked until the first watch of the night passed. At that time according to previous arrangement, the councillor came and when he knocked at the door, the kotwal asked the girl who it was and was very much frightened to hear it was the king's councillor and asked where he could hide himself. She then smeared molasses all over him, poured water on him and covered his body with cotton wool. Thereafter she fastened him to the window. After that the councillor came in and began to talk. She gave him some milk and water and so the second watch of the night passed. After that the king's prime minister came and knocked at the door. The councillor asked the girl who it, was and when she told him, he was exceedingly alarmed and asked where he could hide. She told him she had placed the kotwal in the window and covered him with cotton wool and made a frightful object of him. Then she covered the councillor with the mat and opened the door to the prime minister. He came into the house and sat down on the stool and as before, the girl talked with him till the third watch of the night passed. Then the king himself came and knocked at the door and the prime minister inquired, who it was and as soon as he heard he was very much frightened and asked where he could hide, as there was danger to his life. So the girl took him near the frightful looking kotwal and put him under a screen of bamboo and then opened the door to the king. The king came in and talked to the girl. Meanwhile, the councillor from beneath his mat and prime minister from behind the screen, seeing the hideous form of the kotwal became extremely frightened. Just at that moment, the king who happened to be looking around the house saw the kotwal and said, "What is that fastened there?" The girl replied, "Oh! there is a young rakshasa tied there". As soon as the kotwal heard that he lept out and the king seeing him thought, "He will eat me"; the councillor thought, "He will eat me"; the prime minister thought, "He will eat me"; so they all, one after the other, ran away to their own houses and the kotwal also went back to his house.

From the above example, it is amply clear that even the socially contemporary events found a place in the sculptures of that era. Such a tradition of story-telling continues even today in our country. Many examples can be found in paintings, terracotta sculptures in the temples during the medieval period. But we have fewer examples of wooden sculptures depicting such types of stories in our country such as Swaminarayan temple at Kalupura, Ahmedabad. The main reason for the disappearance of these sculptures lies in the nature of the wood itself, which is perishable by nature. Even today, some remains of these sculptures are still available for the study of these traditions.

The Swaminarayan temple was built in the year 1822. The temple records are still available in its office for confirmation. The *Sabhamandapa* portion in the front of the main shrine was constructed during 1856-1871. At this juncture when records are available, it is needless to furnish any other historic piece as corroboratory evidence for its identification and confirmation.

Events contemporary to the period of construction of the *Sabhamandapa* of the temple had a deep-rooted impact upon the minds of the people and thus the artist as well. They were the eyewitnesses of the events of their time.

The preservation and continuity of Indian art remained intact due to the great tradition of *Guru-Sishya parampara*, i.e. teacher-student tradition. Even today, the classical traditions of dances, paintings, sculptures remains preserved in India. So, the tradition of story-telling through the sculptures seems to have been continuing from the Buddhist *Jataka* in stone to the wooden sculpture of Kalupura temple.

Rightly, the subject matter of Buddhist *Jataka* panel and its identification, as found in sculptures throughout the world are well supported by the script. But the decipherment of the wooden panels carved at Kalupura *Sabhamandapa* temple struts depends upon the contemporary happenings before such scripts came into existence. In the case of the former, the *Jataka* story might have taken place, probably, first in the form of literature and then subsequently these might have transformed in the form of stone. Or may be even the other way round. But, in the case of the latter, entirely the reverse situation comes into notice and observation. On the wooden panels of the *Sabhamandapa* of Swaminarayan temple of Ahmedabad, it is observed that probably, the incidents first captured the memory of the people and then got into the second form, i.e. script, paintings and so on. The people of those times had seen the occurrences taking place before their own eyes, which the artists executed in their works. In due course of time, many books on the first war of Indian independence came into being which describe many events, both known and unknown, like exodus of people, disturbances in trade, punishments, socio-economic fluctuations and various other subjects. The importance of these wooden sculptures of this *Sabhamandapa* lies in its contemporariness and coded evidences, as recorded by the eyewitnesses. In the light of the above thoughts, the decipherment of these sculptures is studied here with references from the Buddhist era in the latter half of the 19th century.

THE FIRST WAR OF INDEPENDENCE AT SHRI SWAMINARAYAN TEMPLE

The tumultuous periods of Indian history marked the blending of ideas to produce the best of policies and principles. The Swaminarayan sect of Gujarat dawned during the first half of the 18th century when the state was passing through a turbulent phase, best explained by Sir John Malcolm as the period when "literally no government existed". It was the time when the British were manoeuvring to consolidate their political powers so far gained. The British East India Company had established a trading enclave at Surat since 1759 and shared a certain degree of political power with the Nawab of Surat. A little later the Gaikwads of Baroda disassociated themselves from the Maratha Confederacy, accepted British protection and established an independent court of their own at Baroda. The first quarter of the 19th century thus witnessed a slow but steady progress in the political and military influence of the British in greater Gujarat.

Gujarat played a significant role during the first war of Indian independence (1857) keeping pace with the rest of the country. Parts of Gujarat namely, Ahmedabad, Khera, Bharoch, Panchmahals, Manikantha, Revakanta and Okhamandala had risen in revolt against the British rule. The incident of cartridges coated with fat of cow and pig that had caused ripples of discontentment is well documented. The British policy had, by and large, reduced the smaller chieftains to rubbles, which became one of the major causes of discontentment among the native rulers.

News of military uprising at Nasirabad, Nimuch, Indore, Jhansi and Mhow against the British rule spread throughout the country like a wildfire and affected Ahmedabad which also followed suit in quick succession. The foremost soldiers of the first war of independence marched with indomitable spirit to Ahmedabad through Indore–Mhow road. Little did they know that their spirit, courage and determination would soon wane. Among these brave soldiers were the firebrand torch-bearers of the insurrection like Govindrao Gaikwad, Bhausahib Pawar, Bhosla Raja, Niyalchand Zaveri and Maganbhai Baniya. Tatya Tope bifurcated his army in December 1858 and started moving towards Ahmedabad with the intention of meeting the friendly forces and deciding on the next course of action. On 16 December 1858, Tatya Tope marched in the direction of Banswada. On the fateful day of 7 April 1859, Mansingh, the ill-famed king of Marwar betrayed the trust of Tatya Tope and got him apprehended by the British who took him by surprise. Tatya Tope, the great son of the nation was hanged on 18 April 1859. According to common belief, which persists in Gujarat, a monk who resembled Tatya Tope was apprehended by the British, while Tatya Tope continued to live in the guise of Taheldas, at Navsari in Gujarat. Taheldas alias Tatya Tope died in 1902. However, definite evidence is needed to establish this belief as a fact.

A major setback came in June 1880 when the forces of the Peshwa of Pune were routed and he was forced to negotiate a settlement with the British wherein the rights of the Gaikwads of Baroda were confirmed and the territory of Kathiawar was ceded to the British. Thus, Gujarat was virtually divided into two parts during the British rule. One merged with the Bombay Presidency under the direct administration of the British and the other was allowed to be ruled by the native rulers under the supervision of the British Residency through Political Agents. The British directly controlled the districts of Ahmedabad, Bharoch, Khaira, Panchmahals and Surat being under the Bombay Presidency. The state of Baroda and a number of other small native states were governed by the British through Residents and Agents. As mentioned before, the second half of the 19th century witnessed the huge assembly of the Maratha army under the leadership of Tatya Tope and the Rani of Jhansi. The indomitable fighting spirit of the Maratha army and their subsequent defeat at the hands of the British finally culminated into the posting of British Political Agents in the court of Indian States, thus resulting in the spread of British empire in India. Tatya Tope, the Maratha chieftain was declared a fugitive by the British. The cruelty, the severe punishments imposed by them on the poor natives, the relegation of independent native rulers to a secondary status after the British Residents and Agents appointed in their courts, suppression of the natives and the breaking of Maratha Confederacy left an everlasting impact on the minds of the Indians.

It was during this reorganisation and realignment of forces and systems that Ahmedabad awakened from its slumber to understand the implication of imperialism and alien rule. Hargovind Das Kantawala and Ambalal Desai started a movement for buying and selling Swadeshi goods (*jagaran* movement) at Ahmedabad (*History of Gujarat* by S.B. Rajyagyor, pp. 418-20).

Under such a political scenario when the nation was passing through a period of psychological agony, physical bondage, spiritual silence and when the freedom of expression seemed a distant dream, Swami Shahjananda and his devotees established a sect of Swaminarayan on fourfold principles, i.e. the anthropic, cosmological, devotional and iconography. He devoted himself to the reformation of the prevalent religious fabric through Swaminarayan bhakti sect. The number of his followers grew rapidly. This attracted the attention of Sir John Malcolm, who wished to have a large number of followers through Swamiji. The two visionaries met at Rajkot and the deliberations recorded have been preserved in the inscriptions on marble slabs fixed at the Swaminarayan temple of Rajkot. These are symbolic of the conjunction of political changes with religious reforms in Gujarat (William Raymond Brady, in "A New Face of Hinduism", *Swami Narayana Religion*, Cambridge Press, 1884, p. 24).

After Swami Shahajananda, the sect was divided in two branches, one being at Vadthal and the other at Ahmedabad. The principal preachers or the Acharyas of the Ahmedabad diocese have been Acharya Ayodhya Prasad (1826-68), Acharya Keshav Prasad (1868-90), Acharya Purushottam Prasad (189-1901), Acharya Vasudev Prasad (1901-37),

Acharya Devendra Prasad (1937-1969) and Acharya Tejendra Prasad (1969-continuing) and H.H. Lalji Maharajshri, Koshlendraprasad Maharajshri who have been the successors to the holy seat.

The temple architecture of Swaminarayan temple of Ahmedabad belongs to the mixed school of Indo-Mughal style initiated in Gujarat during the 19th century, as indicated by Malligon. There are three central shrines called *Shikhar Mandapas* because they have three large domes or *shikharas* over these shrines. The main gateway of each shrine is marked by a tall and elaborately decorated temple tower. The entire temple complex is surrounded by a *prakara*-wall with three entrances in three different directions. The temple has a large open compound generally used to feed birds. The main shrine of the deity occupies the central place in the compound. The shrine building is constructed over a high plinth approachable by a staircase marked with shrines on the side. Various designs ranging from lotus forms to bird figures, sketches of animals, humans and gods like Ganpati and Hanumana can be seen all over the temple. The front portion of the main shrine faces a large open yard surrounded by a *Sabhamandapa* in L-shape on three sides of which one side is in regular use for religious discourses and the second one is used as office for the temple administration.

On the *Sabhamandapa*, there are twelve pillars with beautiful carvings. The pillars sixth, seventh, eighth, ninth, tenth, eleventh and twelfth have carvings of *Ganesha Vyala*, goddesses, lions, parrots, human figures, lotus petals and scrolls. Of these the seventh and sixth pillars have carvings on three sides each and the last one has carvings only on one side which is the subject of this study.

At the first glance, all the carvings on the wooden struts appear as beautiful motifs to the viewers. However, a careful examination and observation of these carvings, keeping in mind their contemporary historical background, reveals some remarkably different facts and events hidden beneath the outer lustre of these carvings.

Each and every pillar of the *Sabhamandapa* is intricately carved with images of the gods and goddesses on the front portion of each strut. The strut is a part of the pillar, which joins the roof and acts as a support.

10. Yavamajhakiya—Jataka

11. Pillar No. 6 (Front)

12. Pillar No. 6 (Left)

13. Pillar No. 6 (Right)

14. Pillar No. 7 (Front)

15. Pillar No. 7 (Left)

16. Pillar No. 7 (Right)

17. Pillar No. 8 (Front)

18. Pillar No. 8 (Left)

19. Pillar No. 8 (Right)

20. Pillar No. 9 (Front)

21. Pillar No. 9 (Left)

22. Pillar No. 9 (Right)

23. Pillar No. 10 (Front)

24. Pillar No. 10 (Left)

25. Pillar No. 10 (Right)

26. Pillar No. 11 (Front)

27. Pillar No. 12 (Front)

These struts of the *Sabhamandapa* are important from the point of view of architectural study of the temple. Almost all of these struts are carved in different manner and with various designs. The wooden craftsmanship of the objects displayed here, marks the zenith of the history of wooden architecture that should be preserved for posterity as a part of national wealth. The pillars of the *Sabhamandapa* which are at the northern end of the temple, have been selected for the study. From the main entrance, one has to move to his left up to the end of the building located on the western side to reach the *Sabhamandapa.* The counting of the pillars for this study is from the left to the right of the viewers. There are carvings on three sides of each and every strut. The carvings on these three sides, i.e. front, left and right positions have to be studied and described separately but collectively. All the seven pillars, which bear a fully carved strut each, are important from the point of study as they bear some historical evidences, which need to be correlated and corroborated with historical facts.

The front side of the strut on the sixth pillar starts with a *Garuda* figure sitting on a snake, which is mounted over a lotus at the base. The stem arising from the lotus bud-throne has petals rising in succession. The petals are shown as parts of the main stem of lotus scroll petals, which bear a Maratha warrior figurine with a sword each. These Maratha warriors appearing on each side of the stem are represented as leaves of the main stem. This decoration continues up to the top of the strut that is about 5′ (approx.) in length and 3.5' (approx.) in breadth. At the terminating point of the lotus bud scroll, there is a representation of a lion as *vahana* of the goddess Durga above. Goddess Durga has been carved with four hands, with the right upper hand holding a trident and the left upper hand holding a snake. The lower two hands are shown as playing a veena. Her face shows marks of strain and her mood disturbed. Her hair is shown scattered and messy, but the representation of a small head over this Durga figurine is shown beautifully. Probably, this was the representation of goddess Shakti. According to the Hindu mythology, no figurine of goddess Durga or Jagdamba is shown holding veena and a snake simultaneously. The snake has been represented in many icons of local goddesses, but no image of Durga is seen with a veena as exhibited here. In contrast to the Hindu mythology, this is a unique and unusual image. Some images of the goddess with mixed characteristics have been reported previously but sporadically. The artists who were responsible for the carvings probably had some intention behind selecting such types of representation. Probably, the artists selected this style of goddess Durga to symbolically represent some lady or some high dignitary of times. It would be appropriate to trace such a royal luminary of Indian history of that era who might have ruled with full sovereignty and an army of her own.

The portion of the strut on the right side needs thorough and minute scrutiny. Here, there is a beautifully carved horse running with a lady adorning a crown in collapsing position. The parrots on this panel are shown in an offensive and pecking mood. The first parrot is placed near the crown of the fallen queen and shown pecking her veil. The second is shown at the bottom of the falling horse. The third parrot is shown attempting to peck the hoof of the left foreleg of the falling horse. The images of the horse with the queen and the parrots are succeeded by a nude female figurine with scattered hair. On the naked *jangha* (thigh) of her body a parrot is shown perched with its head facing rearward. The figure of this naked woman is followed by a representation of a lion in a furious and attacking posture. The lion has been shown as gnawing the hand of the lady carved above. The lady figurine bears a shield in her right hand and a sword in the left, this was probably a historical fact that took place during the war of 1857.

The left side of the same strut bears a beautiful carving of a *Gajavyala* figurine which is shown as rising from the lotus scroll and is followed by images of male and female warriors in a series from the bottom to the top. A female warrior carved at the top is shown in action with a naked sword. She has been shown as wearing a Maharashtrian *dhoti, patal* and *kanchltki* or blouse. Here the parrots are shown at the rear side of the panel busy pecking at the stem of the lotus scroll. The horse carved at the top is in a rising posture without its rider. It is as if the rider had been slain or killed while in action. A Maratha soldier playing a *carnatte* (Tutari), war flute or a trumpet is indicative of a war scene. A collective study of the panel in correlation with one another is needed to decipher the underlying significance of this art form, which clearly depicts a scene of war that the artist might have witnessed by chance. The artist has deliberately selected these motifs not just to decorate the strut, but to give a hint to the viewers on some historical events of his era that left a lasting impression on the Indian historical panorama and the memory of contemporary Indians. An attempt will be made in the conclusion to trace and correlate the depictions of these motifs with contemporary historical facts and events.

On the strut at the front of the seventh pillar we find a similar representation from the bottom to the top, similar to that of the sixth pillar with an exception in the design of the figurine at the top which is a lion-headed warrior. A representation of a *Garuda* figure with scroll-petals of soldiers dressed in Maratha style are depicted here. Interestingly, two parrots each sitting on each shoulder of the warrior are also depicted here. Out of these two parrots, one is seen holding a lotus bud in its beak. This representation has been carefully selected by the artist. On the seventh pillar, the figure of a lion-headed man appears to be one of the mythological figures. In Sanskrit and in almost all Indian languages, a man who is the bravest among the braves is termed as *Narasimha* or *Narakeshari*. Probably the artist might have desired to portray the bravest man of contemporary Indian history through this carving. However, it needs further study and examination through an analysis of the contemporary history to establish and confirm this fact.

On the left strut of the seventh pillar, there is the depiction of *Gajashardula* at the bottom succeeded by Maratha soldiers in aggressive postures rising out of the lotus scroll. The parrots here are shown in two postures, one pecking at the knee of a Maratha soldier and the second pecking the stem of a lotus scroll. It appears that the parrots appearing in pecking mood perched upon the head of the lady are carved deliberately by the artist to hint at some important event. A royal lady of this period, who was practically holding a kingdom, was being troubled by these parrots, which can be identified in this particular piece of work. She is carved as leisurely resting in one posture with troubling parrots and in rage with a sword in the second posture. The female warriors on the top are shown engaged in a fierce battle. It clearly mobilises our thought that the parrots might have forced her to retaliate with the sword. If we corroborate this depiction with some historical fact, we will surely be able to identify this piece of art.

The right side of the strut on the seventh pillar has been carved with a figurine succeeded by Maratha soldiers with a *Garuda* figure with folded hands. A parrot is carved in a posture as if pecking the *Gajashardula*, the *Garuda* resting on its right foot placed upon the tail of the parrot. Above it, the figure of Hanumana resting on a corpse with the tail of the lion, i.e. the *vahana* of the goddess over its belly is suggestive of the union of the goddess and her faithful leader. The corroboration of this carving with the historical data of that era will reveal its identification. At the top, there is a carving of a beautiful image of the goddess sitting on a lion with a sword and a shield and shown as waking the lion by her hand. It appears mind that the artist might have selected the medium of lotus scroll and birds for a symbolic representation of some historical facts of his era. In the concluding chapter, an attempt has been made to logically analyse all possible historical facts and to arrive at the most appropriate conclusion.

Figurines of three parrots are shown at the bottom of the strut in the front of the eighth pillar. Out of these parrots, one is seen resting on the lap of the king seated on the throne and the other two are shown guarding him. At the top, the parrots are shown as surrounding the throne of a queen who is also being guarded by two of these parrots. The lotus scroll stem is carved as a knotted one and the parrots are shown gossiping with each other.

On the left strut of the eighth pillar, six parrots are shown along with a Maratha warrior holding a *Rajadanda* (the state symbol or symbol of authority) in his hand in a *tribhanga* posture and in a resting mood. The second parrot appearing at the neck of the *Gajavyala* succeeds the figure of a Maratha warrior. At the top, the parrots are shown as being fed by some half-clad Maratha gentry in sitting position over the head of the *Gajavyala*. Probably, the artist might have had a desire to carve some contemporary incident in this scene. Before carving these figurines, the artist might have thought of giving an extraordinary status to the parrots by showing one of the parrots on the lap of the king on the throne, another parrot as guarding him and yet another on the neck of the *Gajavyala*. By designing and arranging the parrots in such a way, the artist might have thought of conveying some contemporary happenings.

On the right side, there are the figures of five parrots along with a crane, a Maratha warrior and a *Gajavyala* figurine. The parrots at the bottom are shown as pecking a lotus scroll stem. The second parrot appearing at the neck of the *Gajavyala*, succeeds the figure of a Maratha warrior. The selection of a crane-like bird holding the feet of a Maratha warrior squatting over the head of the *Gajavyala* is suggestive of some inner message. The artists have been very careful in highlighting and selecting proper symbols for their works to convey the exact meanings of the message in their minds.

The front part of the strut on the ninth pillar is a mere reproduction of the eighth pillar. But the position of the parrots at the bottom differs from that of the eighth pillar in which parrots are shown in different moods like gossiping and watching. On the ninth pillar, the parrots are carved as if they are aiming towards the neck of the king on whose lap they are resting. Again, it is the ability of the sculptor, to select and depict the selective mood of the birds for conveying the appropriate meaning of their art. The position and the meaning they desired to highlight by the carvings of the parrots on the eighth pillar might be to show their conspiracy against the king while sitting on his lap. In the case of the ninth pillar, the parrots are carved aiming towards the neck of a king to show their hidden ambition of harming him. While corroborating both the deciphered meanings expressed above through the position and posture of the parrots, we are sure to assess and establish the correct zeal of their art with a clear establishment of the historical fact of that time.

Only the right side of the ninth pillar has some peculiarities. Here, there are the figures of eight parrots below the figure of a Maratha soldier who is shown as holding an inverted weapon in his right hand and a shield in his left as if he is about to commit suicide. Just below this figure, two parrots are shown pecking a lotus scroll stem. The parrots on the top are depicted as gossiping and conspiring against the *Gajavyala* figure. Figures of two other parrots are also depicted here, of which one is sitting over the neck of the *Gajavyala* figure and the other placed above the head of this figure, is holding the left foot of a preceding Maratha soldier with its claws while simultaneously holding a lotus bud in its beak. The artist appears to have made an effort to hint at some important event of Indian history of his period which can only be deciphered after a thorough study and examination of major historical events at the time of construction of this temple and its woodcarvings (i.e. 1856-71).

A figure of a Maratha soldier holding a sword with both hands and resting with crossed legs is carved. Beneath this Maratha soldier, a parrot is shown pecking a Lotus and another shown on the other side is attempting to peck another lotus. Above it, two parrots are shown on each side, each holding a lotus scroll knot of the main stem in their beaks. Two other parrots are shown perpendicularly above these two having a flower knot in their beaks underneath the feet of the Maratha soldier. A pair of Maratha soldiers is also carved, apparently in sitting postures, one on either side of the front part of the strut holding each other's hands. At the shoulder portion of this Maratha soldier, one parrot is shown having a scroll knot in its beak. On the front side of the strut on the tenth pillar, is carved a Maratha soldier holding a sword in both the hands and standing in a cross-legged position above the *Garuda* figure depicted at the base of the strut. Carving continues towards the tip in an unbroken sequence. Just on the top of the Maratha soldier, a lotus scroll stem with a rope having five knots can be seen. These knots have been arranged in succession and are held in position by two parrots standing on the sides at each stage. Two Maratha soldiers in sitting position while shaking their hands can be seen over the lotus scroll. Two other parrots are also shown sitting on the lap of these soldiers busily pecking at their knee. The figure of a king holding a sword in his right hand and a shield in his left with a parrot on his lap is depicted sitting on a lotus throne over the figures of soldiers.

On the right side of the strut, a parrot is portrayed holding a knot of the lotus in its beak at the bottom. The artists have carved only the hind portion of the *Gajavyala* figure at this spot as if they wanted to show that the animal was running away. This depiction is succeeded by the carving of the figure of a British soldier kneeling on his left knee and holding a gun in his left hand at a later stage but in the middle of the strut. A roaring lion places its paw on the soldier's right foot and knee, as if seeking shelter by appearing to whisper into the right ear of the soldier. Another British soldier below the lion has been carved aiming at the same lion with his gun. Above these figures is carved a *Gajavyala,* above which appears the figure of a lion. The lion at the top has been shown patting a parrot with its left forepaw. The carvings on this pillar appear to be a vivid portrayal of some contemporary historical event, which is analysed in the concluding chapter.

Three beautifully carved parrots on the strut of the left part of the tenth pillar have been depicted. The parrot at the bottom is busy holding the stem of the lotus. By the side of the hind portion of the *Gajavyala,* the figure of a half-clad Maratha royalty is carved by the artist. The second parrot is depicted above the head of the half-clad Maratha royalty as though keeping the whole situation under continuous surveillance. The seat of the half-clad Maratha royalty is shown as mounted over the head of the monkeys. The entire contemporary happenings of that era might have attracted the artists to concentrate their attention on a deliberate choice of the subject and befitting objects for portraying this subject at a specific and appropriate spot in their works. The figure of a British personality is depicted sitting on a chair in the middle portion of the strut in succession to the hind portion of the *Gajashardula.* This British gentry sitting on the chair is shown listening to the roaring lion that stands to his left. This lion standing on its hind feet reaches up to the ear of the British gentry and differs in posture and gesture in a clear contrast to a similar depiction on the right side. The *Gajavyala* figure is again shown succeeded by the lion at the top, patting the parrot.

If these figures are corroborated with the history of modern India along with the contemporary happenings in the society and are presented in relation to the historical perspective through a thorough study of the meaning of these depictions, then it would reveal an eye-opening account. The carvings show a direct evidence of British annexation and their policy of that period. The artists came out from the extreme fear of the existing state of affairs and dared to give at least some concrete clue about their intention behind the selection of such symbols for their work.

The front part of the strut on the eleventh pillar is almost a replica of that of the tenth pillar. However, the figures on the left are different.

At the left part of the eleventh pillar, there is the depiction of two half-clad Maratha gentry at the rear of the *Gajashardula* figurine which are designed purposefully to portray the Marathas as a waning political and economic entity. A second uprising *Gajashardula* figure is succeeded by two parrots, one is at its trunk and the other is sitting over its head. Both these parrots are placed under the front and rear feet of the top lion. However, at the front, the parrot under the right forepaw of the lion above appears as being patted by the lion. This is a peculiar scene but in accordance with the intention of the artist to depict the then social and political scenario of the entire nation through their art.

On the right side of this strut, the figure of a British soldier sitting on a chair and being guarded by another British soldier is depicted on the back of the *Gajashardula* figure. Another figure of a *Gajashardula* is succeeded by a lion at the top with a parrot under its left paw, similar to those of the tenth pillar and that on the left side strut of this pillar.

The sequence of exhibition of these woodcrafts end at the twelfth pillar which has figures only on its right side because of its positioning at the *Sabhamandapa* of this historic temple. The figure of the Lord Hanumana with a lady beneath his right foot is carved on the twelfth pillar. The figure has a club in the left hand and the right hand holds his right leg upwards so that the lady beneath can be saved from being trampled. The figure of the lady beneath appears to be a corpse. This fact is further supported by her fixed gaze and her extra wide open eyes. Here again, two parrots are depicted as observing him from above. The figure of the Lord appears to be tied with an iron chain around his waist. Probably this symbolises some historical fact. However, the significance of this representation can be appreciated through the study of mythological background and its relevance to contemporary historical events.

In almost all languages especially in Indian languages, each and every word is used for conveying three different meanings, i.e. *yatartha* or *pratyaksha* (as it seems and really is), *laksanartha* or *paroksha* (symbolic use of the word to convey some hidden meaning) and thirdly the same word can be used in the satirical sense or *vyangartha* (satirical). The same word can be used under different circumstances to convey distinctly different meanings. Particularly in the cases of *laksanartha* and *vyangartha,* words are used to convey a concealed connotation.

The same phenomenon about triple usage of words and symbols is equally and aptly applicable to art, literature and culture as well. There are numerous examples where the creator (be he an artist, a writer, a painter or a performer) has to use symbols as a medium for expressing his inner feelings or subdued emotions or suppressed anguishes. At times, compelling social circumstances may restrain the expression of one's spontaneous feelings for which he may have to take the help of a cover to express himself in such a concealed manner that only the appropriate person can decipher and understand the underlying meanings. Many artists have used symbols as a medium for expression while protecting themselves so that they may escape the brutalities of unforeseen diabolic consequences. Such dual meanings in artistic expressions have their own role to play in adverse circumstances.

The major difference between the art and literature lies not in the expression but in the restrictions of the scope of the use of the word and objects. The poet or author enjoys the freedom to express himself with the substitute words up to the zenith of his intuition. The playwright or an actor or a musician or a painter enjoys lesser degree of freedom in comparison to literature. The sound and its stress along with the facial expression of an actor and musician becomes successful in conveying the exact instinct to the appreciator. The sculptor and the carver need to preconceive and be more exact in their selection of symbols to be used in their works so that they may suit their objectives and intention in a soothing and appreciable manner.

The term *pratyaksha* stands for *paroksha* reference, e.g. "the lotus stands for water and leaf stands for the earth". Lotus and leaf conjointly mean the water (possibility) and the earth (ground) in metaphysical references. Evidently, it is not necessary that the *pratyaksha* and *paroksha* should be sensibly distinct. The actual lotus leaf laid down upon the altar of fire has no meaning of its own; it is merely a datum with respect to which we can have only an estimated or effective knowledge. In other words, it is used only as a reference for some other tangible or intangible substance hidden underneath the outer coating.

The famous *Sabhamandapa* on the western edge of the Swaminarayan temple was constructed within a span of fifteen years (approx.) between 1856 and 1871, when the British were busy in mercilessly consolidating their political power in India. They had even suppressed the freedom of expression of the natives. The atrocities committed by the British and the patriotic spirit of the freedom fighters who laid their lives for the cause of the nation are well documented. The names of the British soldiers who were killed in action during this period have been engraved over the epitaphs of their graves but the names of Indian soldiers who succumbed to the cause of the motherland are difficult to trace although they were countless in number. The Indian peasantry in general had to face day-to-day difficulties in the absence of proper administration. On the economic front, despite being an agricultural economy, the masses were on the verge of starvation. Trade became unsafe and economically not viable. The social life experienced instability and insecurity. The effect of war snatched the means of livelihood from the people. The judiciary stood prejudiced to the interest of the common people. The small zamindars and local chieftains became helpless before the rising cruel and immoral power of the British. This total state of anarchy created a fear psychosis in the minds of the common man. This could be the possible reason why the artist or the engraver might have decided to camouflage his works of art through such symbolic representations on the struts of the pillars in the *Sabhamandapa.*

Works of art are mirrors of contemporary society which reflect the prevailing thoughts, religion, philosophy, cults and culture, social customs, rituals and usage pursued by the inhabitants of that era. In

India, such works of art forms part of a rich commentary on the people who inhabited this soil during different periods. Such architecture portrays how they lived, how they felt, what their ideas were about the divine, the events and the people, how they worshipped and fought and what they created. These are extensive and wide ranging which can be distinctly marked from the now available architectural monuments, sculptures, carvings, images, paintings and other minor arts. The tempo and centre of this creative activity changed during successive periods but the spirit behind such aesthetic endeavours was purely indigenous and peculiarly Indian.

A formal study of a particular piece of woodcarving would only be called complete if the nut could be successfully cracked and the inner thalamus is opened to the outer world. In other words, such a study is said to have achieved fulfilment if an objective interpretation of the soul underneath the outer rind is successfully made. Objects of woodcarvings are dumb by themselves but they stand as a symbol for some inner purpose, which needs to be revealed and appreciated.

Such a formal study needs step by step analysis. One has to put himself in the shoes of the creator of these carvings before undertaking such a study. The next step is to analytically deduce the most probable theme or meaning which could have been possibly expressed in such a concealed manner. Art is abstract but it is significant with its sense and purpose when the message conveyed by the artist through such an art is understood and appreciated by those for whom it is created. The aim of the artist is said to have been achieved if the observer can fully appreciate the historical and cultural purpose of such woodcarvings. The quest of discovering the underlying meaning leads to the study of art of symbolism, e.g. lotus, stem, parrot, serpent and *Gajavyala* in this form of art.

Having identified themes or subjects, the artist might then have moved to select the rhythm and measure such as symmetry, harmony, grouping, proper relationship of the main figure with its constituents and composition which determine the various elements of beauty. The cosmos with its individual objects presents an ideal model for the artist which he expects to portray not so much objectively but through a mental and intellectual language which would make a direct appeal to the observer's mind through the senses.

The supreme value of the art of woodcarving lies in its potential to form a bridge between human mind and the matter.

In India, the art of woodcarving reflects a true relationship between idea and life in the right spirit. It fulfils the need of the hour. It is a special form of art, which enriches the very means and purposes of art and portrays a synthesis of events those which are dearer to the common man.

Prevailing socio-political situation of the area might have forced the intelligent woodcarvers to express themselves through appropriate and selective symbols depicted on pieces of wood. They have chosen lion, monkey, *Gajavyala* and horse among animals and parrot, *Garuda* and crane among birds to symbolically express their version about contemporary happenings of the then society and its political fabric. They have also selected lotus scroll flowers along with a chain as symbols. In order to publicise their message widely, they have given these carvings a religious, floral and faunal touch so that such carvings instantly hit the minds of the common man who would serve as the propagator of the message hidden underneath the outer pomposity of colours. Being conscious of the religious sentiments of common people, they made every endeavour to correlate their thoughts with religious anecdotes thus enabling such art to be passed down from generation to generation as a proud possession. This would also enable the future generations to know the views of their ancestors.

SYMBOLS INTERPRETED

Lotus Scroll and Bud

The most noticeable feature of these pillars is the extensive and extravagant display of lotus along with stems and petals. On all pillars except on the twelfth, there are representations of lotus scrolls in one form or the other.

On the strut of the sixth pillar, a lotus scroll has been carved starting from Garuda figurine at the bottom up to the bottom of the topmost figurine. Each and every petal of the flower represents a Maratha soldier with a weapon under the command of the goddess on top.

The lotus as a symbol of mythic epicentre of power has been widely used by Greeks in their literature and art. It represents resurrection too. Lotus has also been used as an auspicious symbol on which goddess Lakshmi, the goddess of wealth rests. Lord Vishnu, the protector of the universe is also shown with lotus buds. Indian mythology not only recognises the lotus as a symbol of wealth and power but also presents wide depiction to represent these. Therefore, being conscious of the religious sentiments of common Indians, the artist might have selected lotus to represent statehood, principality, sovereignty and kingdom. Every petal of the flower depicted on the front part of the sixth pillar represents an armed Maratha soldier in a camp under the command of the goddess sitting at the top. This is further accounted for in the conclusion.

Similar depictions exist on the seventh pillar with the only difference that the figure at the top is represented by *Narasimha* or Maratha and not a goddess as exists on the sixth pillar. It is clear from these figures that they represent a second camp under their leader which is clear by the depictions of the lotus scroll. This would be further clarified in the conclusion. On the strut at the left side of the sixth pillar, lotus scroll appears to represent the mother of *Gajavyala,* an auspicious symbol to mark a birth in royalty.

At the bottom of the strut to the left of this pillar, a figure of *Gajashardula* followed by Maratha soldiers in aggressive mood rises from the lotus scroll. From this depiction, it becomes clear that the royalty and army both are represented through a lotus scroll.

Figures on the eighth pillar show the stem of the lotus scroll being pecked by the parrots. It is here that one can see the petals representing Maratha soldiers. This would further help identify the historical context related to such depiction.

A lotus scroll is depicted on the front part of the ninth pillar.

Carving of the stem of this scroll is in the pattern of knots and is shown as being held by the parrots in their beaks from both the sides at the joints. The lotus scroll is shown as being pecked by the parrots. Needless to say that such a depiction shows the gradual decline of Maratha resistance. This will further be correlated with contemporary historical events.

A continuous chain of lotus scroll appears on the tenth pillar with Maratha soldiers presented in a resting mood. Five knots of the lotus scroll, which appear on both the sides, are held by parrots at both the ends as if they are guarding each and every joint of the scroll. It can be safely inferred from this picture that the parrots have raised themselves to a commanding position and that they have become capable of regulating the progress of the scroll, i.e. the Maratha empire. This will further be elaborated in the conclusion.

Such depictions, although strange, yet cannot be said to be wild depictions without a definite meaning. Absence of lotus scrolls and petals on the twelfth pillar appears to be a deliberate work of the artist.

Depiction of petals as soldiers, as mother of *Gajavyala,* as a resting place of Maratha soldiers, oral consumption of lotus petals by parrots, holding the knots of a lotus scroll by the parrots in their beaks appear to have definite significance. A thorough examination is essential to decipher the symbolism embodied in these figures to understand and to appreciate their significance and meaning. It appears that the gathering of soldiers in two different camps, one each under the leadership of a goddess and the *Narasimha* portray two different camps of principality of their time. Pecking of lotus petals and also holding the knots appear to symbolise some major events of contemporary history. At this stage, it would be suffice to say that the lotus scroll has been used to represent a kingdom with a vast army.

Parrot

The figures of parrots in different moods appear on almost all the struts. According to Greek mythology, parrot is a greedy bird and can only be silenced through bribe. This bird is also used to depict horrors of the forces of disruption and acts of politicians. The inherent qualities of the parrot have been considered by the carvers to express their intention through symbolism or *lakshanatha*. Parrot is known to learn the language of human beings. Its colour is appealing and it has a sweet voice too. Such qualities of parrots like speaking sweet words, learning the language of others, migrating from one place to the other with ease and their greediness, might have persuaded the woodcarver to portray such birds in profusion doing different acts in order to convey unpopular acts of some of the contemporary personalities whose qualities resemble those of the parrots.

In the woodcarvings of the sixth pillar to the eleventh pillar, parrots in different postures can be noticed on the struts. Four parrots in pecking postures appear on the left side of the strut, whereas four parrots in various moods like pecking the veil, the horse and sitting on the *jangha* can be viewed on the right side. On the front part of the seventh pillar, two parrots are carved each sitting on each of the shoulders of the *Narasimha* or *Narakeshari* or the warrior figure. One of these parrots is holding a lotus bud in its beak. It is quite noticeable that the parrots are reduced in number on the struts of the seventh pillar in comparison to those on the sixth pillar. On the right strut of the seventh pillar, one parrot is shown on the top, sitting on the chest of a lady figurine whereas another parrot is depicted as pecking the *Gajavyala* figurine at the bottom. On the left strut of the seventh pillar, one parrot is shown as chasing and about to peck a lady-warrior carved in the middle. At a subsequent position, at the top, the parrot has been shown as superseding the lady-warrior and pecking another Maratha gentry. Another parrot at the bottom is carved as pecking at the knee of another Maratha soldier whereas subsequent one is shown attempting to peck some other soldier.

On closely examining the front of the eighth pillar, three figures of parrots can be noticed of which one is resting on the lap of a king seated on the throne whereas the other two are seen keeping a watch over him from the sides. Similarly, two parrots are shown around the throne of a queen, apparently being on the guard. However, five other parrots are carved as gossiping.

The depictions of parrots, a king and a queen in such a manner raises many questions. Why did it become essential for the artist to show a parrot on the lap of the king at the bottom, while two others are shown guarding him simultaneously? Or why did the artist use the symbols of parrots and to represent whom? It appears that the artist has taken the help of symbols to conveniently conceal their identities although it restricts his expressions. What messages do these mute figures convey?

Here, it would be expedient to recall the political scenario of India prevailing during the period when these motifs were carved. This would help in understanding the meanings of these symbolic representations. Retrospection is required to reveal a hitherto closely guarded secret.

An analysis of the prevailing political scenario would help in deciphering the meanings underlying these symbolic representations. It was during the years preceding and succeeding 1857 when Indians lost their freedom of expression that these motifs were carved. The artist might have desired to express his views on contemporary happenings but could not have done so for fear of reprisal. But he had to submit to his intense desire of expressing his disappointment at the happenings around him. This might have forced him to use the guise of symbols to keep his identity concealed while expressing his views through figures. At a time when the status of sovereign Indian kings had been relegated to a secondary status with the British Residency and Agents securing the primary status, that the figure of parrot on the lap of the king was carved. This figure was carved intentionally to convey the higher status of British Residents or Agents in the Indian courts. Parrots keeping guard over the king or the queen could possibly mean the alien watch over native sovereigns.

It is an established fact that the years preceding and succeeding the revolution of 1857 witnessed the appointment of British Residents and Agents in Indian courts. The parrots depicted in these panels are not just decorative pieces to charm the viewers. On the contrary, the significance of portraying motifs of parrots lay elsewhere. Possibly, these motifs were used as symbols to convey some *lakshanartha*, i.e. some hidden meaning. This is clear from the positioning of the parrots, their differing moods and different actions. On the right side of the eighth pillar, parrots, five in number, along with a crane, a Maratha warrior and a *Gajavyala* are carved whereas at the bottom of the same pillar parrots are shown pecking the stem of a lotus scroll and at the bottom of the sixth pillar they are shown pecking the veil of a queen. By displaying carvings of parrots in postures doing such actions, the artist might have intended to convey some significant historical event of his era. An analysis of the political events of that era reveals that British came to India with the intention of trade and to achieve their purpose, they mastered the native languages.

Further, the British had very closely observed the state of affairs persisting in Indian native states and might have desired to gain political mileage from the existing circumstances. The artist of these motifs had a clear intention to symbolically depict this historical fact with the help of the characteristics of parrots.

On front of sixth pillar parrots are shown with a Maratha warrior holding a glib in a *tribhanga* posture and in a mood of resting. The second parrot sitting on the neck of the *Gajavyala* at the top, succeeds the Maratha warrior. The parrots are shown as being fed by a half-clad warrior which is indicative of the intention of the artist to narrate some historical event through such strange symbolic expressions. The artist has successfully carved the socio-political conditions of the then rulers through the use of such symbols. By then, these native rulers had become financial wrecks and were militarily crippled, hence portrayed as half-clad gentry feeding the parrot with their own hands. The second half of the 19th century witnessed that although the Indian rulers had lost all their political and military powers, still they had to feed their alien masters either directly or through Political Agents or Residents. Possibly, this had been the intention of the artist and it is to depict these political and moral downfalls of Indian sovereigns that the artist has successfully and intelligently expressed himself through the use of parrots as symbols on these struts.

On the right side of the strut of the ninth pillar, eight parrots are shown above the figure of a Maratha soldier, who has been shown holding an inverted weapon in his right hand, apparently in a mood to commit suicide and two parrots pecking lotus stems are depicted beneath this figure. By the depiction of a Maratha soldier in a suicidal posture, the artist has possibly desired to convey the sordid status of the Marathas following the war of 1857. Through such sardonic depictions of parrots and the Marathas, the artists desired to convey the consequences of the first war of Indian independence on the Maratha Confederacy.

The parrots shown at the top appear to be gossiping and conniving against the *Gajavyala* figure carved underneath. Two other parrots are also shown of which one is holding the left foot of a Maratha soldier with a lotus bud in its beak whereas the second parrot is shown sitting over the shoulder of yet another Maratha soldier. It appears that the artist has purposefully carved parrots as conspiring, holding the neck of the *Gajavyala* and pulling the leg of a Maratha soldier with its claws while holding a lotus bud in its beak and to that purpose he has achieved success. Through such depictions of conspiring parrots, possibly the artist attempted to convey the desire of the British to gain a higher status over the native sovereigns and reduce them to a subordinate status. Towards the last part of 19th century, the nation witnessed the subordinate status of native princely states with nominal authority. The artist has aptly depicted this by positioning parrots over *Gajavyala* and showing the act of leg-pulling which was the ill-famed policy of the British during this period. Thus, through such motifs, the artist has befittingly described the socio-political fabric of India during the last quarter of the 19th century.

A lotus scroll rises from the base of the strut on the tenth pillar at the front, succeeding the figure of a Maratha soldier holding a sword in both his hands and resting in a cross-legged posture. The lotus scroll stem with a five-knotted rope is shown continuing upwards from above this figure with the knots being held by parrots in their beaks from both the ends. On the same pillar, parrots are shown on the lap of a king sitting on the throne. The artist has repeatedly highlighted the stature of the parrots through which he possibly intended to convey the condition of Indian princely states. Though the sovereign princes were apparently on the throne yet they were in chains held by the

Residents and Agents as symbolically conveyed through the depiction of parrots which show that the real statehood was tightly held by the parrots, i.e. the British.

Gajavyala

The *Vyala* in Indian art is an imported conception, which luxuriated in the extremes of Indian climate. The form of *Vyala* is devised on the basis of deformities of human and animal forms. In literature, it is often termed as *Vikata*. It had been *Gana, Pramatha, Bhuta, Yaksha* and *Rakshasa* in the *Puranas*. The motifs are either used as decorative repertoire in the carving or are used as pleasing forms to reveal a taste that is superb and exhilarating.

The *Vyala* figure used in almost all parts of India is borrowed from Scythian sources through Gandhara art. Almost all medieval temples in India bear this figure in stone architecture. However, the antiquity of *Vyala* can be dated back to the Mauryan period.

Among the medieval temples also, *Vyala* figure has been chiefly used at Virateshwar temple of Sohagpur and Krishna temple of Valam in Gujarat. Figures of *Vyala* also find a place on the pillars of the *torana* in front of *Hastisala* of Vimala Vasahi at Dilwara and Vadnagar. The Baroda gate and two other gates of Dhabora support the *mandala* in the *Prodoli* (strut). The *Vyala* forms of the 10th century temples of Gujarat, for instance, exhibit vertical tensional movements with coquettish ado.

M.S. Dhake in his work *Vyala* figure on "The medieval temples of India", (published under, *Indian Civilisation*, Series 11, Varanasi, 1965, pp. 1, 9) has mentioned that "In South India the *Vyalas* on the temples of Pallava and early Chola period are splendid examples of concentrated energy in a poise, but ready to bounce when an opportunity comes. And that came later when they sprang to action whose manifestation and impact were too violent as seen in the marriage halls of Vijayanagar and early Nayaka authorship".

In the art forms of western India, the *Vyala* figure is often accompanied by a kneeling knight as if engaged in an encounter. The knight is often thrown into action under the spell of terror of a rearing and balancing *Vyala*. In the art of Orissa, the *Vyala* form is most frequently seen on an elephant back. Sometimes the *Vyala* form even appears as if trampling an elephant *Gajakrania*. In Orissa earlier such forms of *Vyala were* termed rather wrongly as *Gajavidhala*. At Alampur and Bhuwaneswar, *Vyalas* are seen tamed or irked by a rider. Normally, they are used as unbridled, autonomous and delimited. In these carvings, the *Vyala* figures have probably been used to show the concentrated energy of the native states of India, ready to pounce instantly at the earliest opportunity.

Lion

Lion figures are carved on the right strut of the sixth and the eighth pillar, left and right strut of the tenth pillar and lastly on the right strut of the eleventh pillar.

The lion in Western mythology is often described as a symbol of physical strength identical to the flow of continuous energy and fertility. It has also been considered as a sign of nobility, real dignity, imperial majesty and supreme animal-hood. In Indian mythology, lion is described as the *vahana* of the goddess of Power or Shakti. It is also considered as a sign of majestic vigour, dignity and as the king of animals for its brutality and fierceness. In the mentioned panels, lions are used as signs of imperial majesty in either way.

Serpent

The snake is characterised as a hissing and biting reptile, which represents cosmic forces in a spiritual creature. It is often used to symbolically represent phallic and sun. It represents fertility and is considered as the Lord of the Underworld having deep wisdom. It also represents a wise animal, which is conscious of all the secrets of life, resurrection and its continuity. At times, it represents strategy, military fame, courage and vigilance in association with an attribute of lust for power.

In Indian mythology, it is described as a spiritual creature associated both with Lord Shiva and Lord Vishnu. It is also known as Sheshnag who holds the Earth on its hood. But, in the carvings of this temple, the artist has probably used the figures of snakes to represent strategy and military power through such symbols.

Crane

A crane is rarely given a place in any art. It is known as a bird of character with a "honey tongue and a heart of gall". It is often found meditating with decisive calmness and quietness with the sole intention of catching fish. The figures of cranes are used to represent such dual characters as calmness with lust.

Monkey

In Indian mythology and literature monkeys are considered as mischievous characters. But in association with Lord Rama, they are considered as the scared soldiers of the Lord. However, monkeys are commonly used to signify the mischievous character of an individual. The Sanskrit literature is full of episodes on monkeys and their efforts are often ridiculously narrated as *markatachesta.*

Hanumana

In Indian mythology, Hanumana is known as the famous son of the Air god or *Vayuputra.* He also represents the *Rudra avatar* and an ardent devotee of Lord Rama. He is the most trusted and sacred lieutenant of Lord Rama. Famous for his outstanding courage, sincerity and loyalty to his master, this monkey-faced god finds a great place in *Puranic* literature of India and it has exerted a tremendous influence over the minds of Indians. Even today, the name Hanumana is used to signify the loyalty and devotion of any person to his master. In *paroksha* and *pratimanam* his name is considered as a synonym to devotion and loyalty.

In India, traditional symbols, whether verbal, dramatic, iconographic or architectural always refer to domains which are unassailable, express those that are inexpressible and fathom those that are unfathomable. In traditional symbolism, the main thrust is directed towards acquiring knowledge about the intangibles and towards knowing the unknown to a certain degree. Symbolism is used to communicate, as far as possible, the nature and the state of the issue in question. Owing to their unbroken tradition, reliable sculptures, written documents of notable antiquity and the rich symbolism developed in all fields of art, these carvings have preserved their continuity for such a long period, which is still effective in a truly significant manner. A study of these carvings would be in the true spirit of such great traditions, events and historical occurrences only if such a study is made from the inside and not from the outside. So, one has to carefully acquaint himself with the historical, traditional and doctrinal concepts of these carvings, to understand the language expressed by these and develop a systematic study with the use of this language, to express precisely the concepts that reveal themselves through the architectural symbolism of these carvings. So, a study of this kind should be conducted with a concern not so much for the formulation of concepts but for exploring the inherent truth. This truth belongs to an order, i.e. properly speaking it belongs to a formulated system and therefore one cannot be affected by the formal differences in the conceptual thinking of different individuals.

Before translating his thought into action, every artist first sows the seeds of such an idea in the fertile soil of his mind for germination. The idea has to grow to a maturing stage in his mind only, so that he is able to present the same before the masses. While he is still at the planning stage, he must decide on the materials needed by him and the sequence of action to be followed to execute his plan. The more he sweats in planning, the less he would labour while execution. He must decide upon the medium that suits him best for the execution of his intended purpose.

Similarly, in woodcarving also, the artist has to decide first the sequence of events that he intends to carve, then decide upon the medium and the postures of the figures to be depicted through such art. A close and careful scrutiny of the woodcarvings, speaks volumes about the strong conviction of the artist to reveal his inner feelings to the outer world. Bearing this in mind, the artist decided to give expression to his feelings through different and divergent but concurrent motifs. The images may be different but they have only one story to relate and that is the struggle for survival of the local populace during the period of the construction of the temple, i.e. 1856-71. The struts of these pillars were carefully chosen to suit his requirements. The figures of paradoxically opposing characters like the legendary *Garuda* and the snake have been displayed side by side over a lotus throne in full bloom. The lotus has been used as a throne or a seat or a base of the strut of every pillar. It has been clearly established that the symbol of lotus stands for the earth and earthly affairs. The characters of a snake do not need any illustration or elaboration. The natural and eternal enmity that exists between the *Garuda* and the snake needs no commentary. This natural hostility between these two foes by birth, has been aptly depicted by the artist to project the enmity between two diametrically opposing forces existing during their period.

Once the historical background of this symbolism is understood, it will then be appreciated as transcending from its particular form to its practical application. While adopting such a point of view, it can be said that all these carved symbolism refer to one definite aspect. The choice of aspect, its form and application will then not be of paramount importance since each of these limiting conditions can be taken as definite. The point of departure is then, so to speak, contingent or peripheral compared to the point of reference and that is essential.

In distinguishing thus a language of symbols from a language of signs, I have in mind the distinctions of symbols and signs carved. A symbolic expression is one that is held to be the best possible formula by which allusion may be made to a relatively unknown thing or event which, however, is nevertheless recognised as existing. The use of any such symbol as the parrot, lion, *Gajavyala,* crane or serpent implies a conviction or tradition and generally a conventional or traditional agreement resting on authority or events. The relatively unknown referent cannot be more clearly represented. A symbol or a sign on the other hand is an analogous or an abbreviated expression for a definitely known thing. Every such tangible object can be indicated or represented through the use of symbols. Even intangibles can be represented although the meanings may not be fully interpreted in their proper perspective.

CONCLUSION

Having closely examined the carvings on the pillars, we note that symbols have been chosen to portray the underlying facts. In this particular form of art, i.e. woodcarving, every bird, animal or plant is used according to its inherent qualities to project those of the others. In other words, each of these symbols is used to convey some hidden meanings to the observers. Let us keep the facts of *paroksha* and *pratimana* use of symbols in our minds and examine the panels carved on these struts.

On the strut at the front of the sixth pillar (bottom), we find a *Garuda* with snake, lotus scroll stem, two *Gajavyalas,* Maratha soldiers with cross-swords arising from the lotus stem as petals, a goddess with trident, snake and veena in her hands and sitting on a lion.

The lotus being the symbol of the epicentre of power, can be correlated with the political power, whosoever might be weaning thus implying a state or a kingdom, a camp either large or small. Simultaneous depiction of petals each representing a Maratha soldier with weapon under the leadership of the goddess above, strengthens the view of a kingdom or a camp which could have been the epicentre of power.

The serpent symbolises strategy and military power. It being in the hand of the goddess denotes authority.

If we correlate the descriptions given in the above paragraphs with the historical events of the period of construction of this *Sabhamandapa,* we find that a kingdom and a camp with an army during 1857, under a lady, was that of the Rani of Jhansi. So it is safe to assume that the depiction at the front of the sixth pillar is a symbolic representation of a princely state of that era. However, this fact will further be corroborated with other symbols for confirmation. On a careful observation of the right strut of the sixth pillar, we find a beautifully carved figure of a lady on horseback adorning a crown, who is about to collapse, is preceeded by the figurine of a nude female with scattered hair. Perched on the naked *jangha* of her body is a parrot looking rearwards. The figurine of this naked woman is preceded by the representation of a lion, in rage. The lion has been depicted as gnawing the left hand of a lady carved vertically above it. A lady figurine appears at the top right hand corner of this strut holding a shield.

The depiction of a number of parrots in different postures on this strut apparently reveals that the figures are used as merely symbols to convey some latent meaning. A parrot is known for its greediness, dishonesty and sweetness of tongue, as one who can imitate the language of others and for its migratory nature. So the artist might have portrayed figures of the parrots to symbolically represent persons in whom these characteristics are apparent. These assumptions find their reflections in the socio-political conditions of the then living populace of that era. If the depictions of parrots are correlated with Indian history, it can be observed that these are reflective of the passive hostility of 1857 existing between the British and the Indian natives. If these depictions with the selection of symbols are corelated with the happenings or incidents of historical significance of the contemporary period of the artist, we can easily conclude that these figures portray the assembly of rival forces, i.e. one under the British and the other under the queen of Jhansi. The only army under the command of a lady during that period was that of Rani Laxmibai.

If we observe the positioning and actions of these parrots, on the panel, we find that they are shown in an aggressive mood and about to peck. One has been placed near the crown of the falling queen and shown as pouncing on her veil. The second parrot has been shown below the falling horse with open beak and about to strike. The third parrot has been shown as pecking the forehoof of the horse.

The artist might have desired to draw larger attention to his depictions and so he carved the figures of parrots in different postures, moods, doing different acts, portraying various human traits such as greediness, dishonesty, capable of imitating other's languages, and pecking. If such actions of these parrots are correlated to any historical character involved therein then the only parallel can be found in various characters of the British. Apparently, these parrots were selected by the intelligent artist to represent the enemies of the queen who were engaged in a moral combat with her. These depictions clearly point to the first war of Indian independence, which had taken place between the native troops and the British in India during 1857.

The carvings at the front and right strut of the sixth pillar clearly illustrate the scene of the deadly battle between the famous Rani of Jhansi with her troops and the British army.

This act is further corroborated by the images on the same pillar. The image of goddess Durga at the top with lion, veena and snake is nothing but a representation of the Rani herself as the captain of the Maratha forces. Although the figure of a child on her back has not been shown, probably because of lack of space, or because of the initial stage of depiction, yet the horse, the crown, the sword, the shield and the style of clothing all point to a royal lady of that period. No other female personality of that period matches the characteristics incorporated by the artist in this figure. Even if a telescopic view of the women of India of this period is taken, then the only parallel to the indomitable spirit, exemplary courage and outstanding leadership displayed through the postures of this figure finds its reflection only in the Rani of Jhansi. Moreover the Maratha style of her regal attire, crown and horse all point to the saga of Rani Lakshmibai.

Some objections may be raised from some quarters about her being represented as goddess Durga. In this context, it can be said that with the ethno-archaeological pattern of our nation, the bravest among the brave ladies is generally termed as Durga. In our literature, the writers or the poets refer to Durga as a synonym for a lady of outstanding valour and exceptional courage. Therefore, the artist chose the image of goddess Durga or Shakti to represent the Rani of Jhansi.

The artist, while carving the image of goddess Durga at the top of the strut has shown her with the lion as her *vahana* or the means of conveyance. Here, it can be seen that the lion has been depicted twice. Although the figure of the lion has been carved in different postures doing different acts in these carvings, yet it can be seen that it is more specifically used as a *vahana* or a beast of burden to carry the lady. The depiction of lion illustrates vigorousness, dignity, ferociousness, fierceness, wilderness, majesty and also as an imperial sign in the carvings of the strut on the sixth pillar, highlighting its mythological significance. At the second place of this strut, the lion can be seen as biting the sword of a lady-warrior. At the right strut of the sixth pillar, the artist has used the lion to indicate the wildness and the fierceness with imperial majesty of the animal as a bitter enemy of the woman-warrior. At the front of the same pillar she is also shown as having four hands, with the right upper hand she holds a trident and a snake with the left upper hand while her two lower hands are busy playing veena. Her face appears strained and her mood disturbed. Her hair is shown scattered and messy. A small and oval female head appears over the forehead of this goddess figure. It is apparent that, the artist has intentionally selected and carved this small figure upon the forehead of this unusual goddess to mark her identity. The small figure of a female's head in sculpture in Indian mythology has been considered as a symbol of Shakti or a spirit. By accepting the meaning of this small head as Shakti and in association with the deeds of the mighty queen of Jhansi of 1857, it hints at the identity of the goddess as the queen of Jhansi.

The artists were definitely well conversant with the Hindu mythology. They had carved this image of unusual iconography with clear depiction of her mood on her face. Each and every line of her face conveys some meaning. They were conscious that only religious motifs have the potential to survive for long duration for obvious reasons and draw instant public imagination. This could be the possible reason why they have depicted the image of goddess Durga to represent someone else as they knew that the personality behind the symbol of goddess Durga could be well identified by the viewers who may react in accordance with the message conveyed through these figures. The carved face of goddess Durga is not as beautiful as the goddess should really be but attempts to enable the viewers to identify the person whom the image of goddess Durga represents.

In the same piece of their work, we find a nude female figure with a parrot sitting on her naked right thigh with its head turned rearwards, thus showing her being politically exploited. This might have been done to show that no moral or ethical outrage of her modesty could have possibly or probably been committed with this mighty lady. The figure of the parrot eyeing rearwards is probably a deliberate act of the carver to indicate the ultimate outcome of the war. The winners, i.e. the British, had although succeeded in the fight yet they still maintained their dignity and morality. The important fact revealed through these motifs is the praiseworthy attitude of the victors, towards the vanquished, i.e. the Rani. So the representation of the British as parrots on this panel is once again appropriate.

It is evident from the historical data of this period that the lady-warrior is the leading lady of the natives engaged in the war with the imperial power. At the right side of the sixth strut, we can see a war scene symbolically carved. During the contemporary period of the artist, there was no other woman-warrior who was engaged in such a fierce battle with the British than the Rani of Jhansi. The sword she held, was picked by the Britishers, at the last moment when she collapsed. The same sword is displayed at the Kumaon Regiment Headquarters in Ranikhet, further, strengthening and establishing the identity of the Rani of Jhansi.

The depiction of *Gajavyala* as another animal figure at the same place is not out of context. On the contrary, it has been used to symbolically represent some facts about contemporary history. Indian mythology is replete with instances where *Vyalas* are used to indicate concentrated potential energy ready to pounce on the enemy at the earliest opportunity. At the base of the sixth strut, two *Vyalas* are carved intelligently and meaningfully to indicate this potential energy of the natives ready to pounce when an opportunity comes.

During the second half of the 19th century (i.e. 1850-1900), the British were busy acquiring and consolidating their territories in India. The depiction of two *Gajavyalas* at the base of this strut is possibly to indicate the huge concentration of the native forces in 1857 against the British. This further strengthens the view that the lady-warrior depicted on this strut is none other than the mighty Rani of Jhansi.

At the right of this strut, the lion is carved and is shown as biting the sword of a woman-warrior. The difference in placement and postures of these two lions convey diametrically different meanings. The figure of the second lion is used to clearly convey the meaning as a royal warrior and not as a *vahana,* as used before. The hostility of the lion engaged in a close quarter battle with the woman-warrior points out the involvement of native women-warriors in the war with the imperial power, symbolically represented as the warring lion. If the, strategic and tactical scenario of the nation persisting during the period of construction of these struts, i.e. the last half of the 19th century is studied with the historical happenings of 1857, it will easily enable us to arrive at the conclusion and identification of these carvings with the Rani of Jhansi as the woman-warrior and the lion as the British. The second corroboratory evidence about the death of the horse just before her demise is well established and described by the historians of that era. In this panel, the artist has also repudiated this fact by depicting the woman-warrior without the horse, which justifies the truth about the incidents associated with the Rani of Jhansi during the first war of Indian independence. So, it confirms that these motifs have full resemblance with the historical and contemporariness of the event of 1857. On the same pillar, below the woman-warrior without the horse, a nude figure of an empty-handed lady has been carved. The nude in art represents a corpse. Probably, this depiction might have been carved in order to show her death.

The right strut of the sixth pillar has four scenes. At one place, the story of that mighty queen and her horse in a collapsing position has been depicted surrounded by the parrots, i.e. the British. The parrots are carved in attacking postures apparently attacking the horse with the rider. In the second place she is shown without the horse and the lion is shown as gnawing one of her hands. In the third place she is shown as a nude corpse. At the fourth place (at the top of the scene), she is shown as acquiring the spiritual status as the goddess on the lion. The corroboration of these figures with the incidents of the contemporary period justifies the assertion that the lady figure is that of the great queen of Jhansi.

A careful retrospection of the political and military scenario of the last half of the 19th century (1850-1900) of the nation, would reveal that the British had acquired and consolidated their power. The British policy of collection of revenue and curtailment of the political power of the native sovereigns overburdened many of the rulers in India. Many history books narrate the causes of the upsurge of the natives against the British. Before 1857, we find many of the small states were waiting for an opportunity to overthrow the British. The Peshwa of Pune, Asitulla Khan of Bengal, Nawab of Oudh, king of Delhi and other smaller and weaker states were waiting to pounce. The selection of the symbol of *Gajavyala* as the native resistance of Indian princes against the British was intelligently and meaningfully represented by the artists on these pillars. They were successful in showing the concentrated energy of the Indian native rulers through their art. So the identification of *Gajavyala* in this panel is the resisting consolidated energy of Indian native rulers.

On the left side of the strut on the sixth pillar, a *Gajavyala* figurine has been carved in uprising posture. The figure of one parrot is depicted at the hind position of the same, attempting to peck the scroll. The second parrot is carved as pecking the scroll leaves and the third one as resting and pecking the scroll and the stem. The fourth parrot seems to be aiming towards the lady-warrior holding an open sword carved at the top. A horse without its rider and a trumpet blower are also carved at this place.

The artist, through the depiction of parrots in different postures, i.e. the British, indulging in different acts impresses upon the fact that a bugle call (blowing the trumpet) is being given to everyone to unsheath their swords (even to the horse which had recently lost its rider). In other words, the artist has indicated the cause best known to him, for the upsurge of the lady displayed at the top.

On the front of the seventh pillar, the carvings start with the figure of a *Garuda* at the bottom, sitting on a snake. A lotus scroll rises vertically from the head of this figure towards the top. The figure of a *Gajavyala* is depicted at the lateral but above the head of this figure. Every leaf of the scroll above the figure of the *Garuda* is represented as a soldier with cross-swords. The scroll culminates at the figure of the *Narasimha* depicted at the top with two parrots on his shoulders. One parrot is held tightly by him whereas the other one has a bud in its beak.

Through the simultaneous depiction of the *Garuda* and the snake with their forces, the artist had successfully carved the rivalry of two forces at war. The assembly of soldiers with crossed swords in one place is shown through the portrayal of leaves arising out of the stem. The person at the command of these forces is depicted at the top with a lion-headed personality highlighting the second camp of native army under a general. History books, give us the description of the one and only unparalleled character then existing in the field of action as Tatya Tope. He was neither a king with any kingdom nor even a general with an army before this war of independence, but his courage, tactics, speed, strategy and inborn qualities of leadership established him superior to many other trained generals. So the artists, intentionally and deliberately, had not carved him with a crown as they intended to show other personalities associated with this event in their work of art, at this place.

The personalities involved in the first war of independence were at least village chieftains, who had every right to wear at least a turban as a crown. A simple clerk or a mere servant in the court cannot decorate his head with a crown. The artist has, deliberately and intentionally chosen a lion's head to decorate this great personality, which is a befitting insignia for Tatya Tope. So it is safely ascertained that the figure depicted as *Narasimha* at the strut of the front part of the seventh pillar is Tatya.

On the right side of the strut of the seventh pillar, a *Gajavyala* figurine has been carved. The figure of a parrot has been depicted as trying to catch the tail of *Gajavyala,* chased by Maratha soldiers in action. On the same panel, the figure of a *Garuda* is shown followed by the figure of the corpse of a lady beneath the figure of Hanumana. One side of this figure is occupied by a beautiful motif of a four-armed goddess with a crown on her head and in a furious mood. She is shown to be holding a sword and a shield respectively in her right and left hands. Of her other two hands, one is seen holding the lion by one of its ears and the other one is invisible. At the top, the figure of a lady is depicted with a parrot on her chest. She is in the posture of trying to get rid of it with her hand. In this panel, the artist has portrayed the parrot and the *Gajavyala* to convey some symbolic meaning.

In the preceding paragraphs, it has been explained that the figures of parrots have been used as symbols for the British and *Vyala* represents the native rulers. So, the parrot pecking at the tail of the *Gajavyala* can be safely interpreted as the Britisher's lust to acquire the territories of the native rulers. This lust of the parrot or the Britishers resulted in the union of native rulers to identify them as their common enemy and organise a huge assembly of Maratha army under the leadership of the goddess or the Rani of Jhansi supported by Hanumana and *Garuda.* All these three symbols paint the great concentration of confederacies under one leader. This follow-up action by the confederate states to assemble themselves under the queen of Jhansi and against a common enemy, i.e. the British, is further elaborated by the act of the goddess being engaged in dispelling the parrot from her chest. In other words, left side of this pillar shows the pre-war scenario of military concentration that the artist might have personally witnessed.

If we view the pre-1857 scenario critically, it can be observed that the forces of the great Tatya Tope, those of Govindrao Gaikwad, Maganbhai and others had all assembled under the mighty queen of Jhansi. Even the intolerable irritation suffered by these local captains has been recorded by the artist through his carvings of a parrot on the chest of the lady at the right side of the seventh pillar.

With this interpretation of such bizarre symbols and motifs, it can be concluded that the British might have played mischief or might have interfered with the authority of the native rulers to such a great extent that these native rulers or chieftains or kings or captains might have been on insurrection to oust the Britishers from their land. These symbols have probably been used to convey this message.

The front part of the sixth pillar apparently shows the second stage of the insurrection of a huge native force under the leadership of the queen ready to pounce on the alien forces at the earliest available opportunity.

The carvings on the strut on the right side of this pillar show the actions of the forces of the native sovereigns and the ultimate outcome of the first war of independence. The history of India during this period and soon after is same as the period of construction of the *Sabhamandapa* (1856-71) so, naturally, the happenings of this period were destined to find their reflection on its carvings. The events associated with Tatya Tope, Govindrao Gaikwad and others occurred on this very soil. Hence it can be inferred that the identifications and meanings supposedly conveyed by these figures and their postures stand on a sound rationale from the point of contemporary history of India. It can be safely assumed that the strut on the sixth to twelfth pillars are carved in memory of the carnage of the first war of Indian independence of 1857.

The carvers had probably felt that they would be doing a great disservice to the nation if they did not carve incidents related with the insurrection of 1857. Therefore, on the strut of the seventh pillar, similar depictions can be observed which might have been carved by the artist from the bottom to the top with the exception of the top figurine that depicts a lion-headed warrior, in order to give vent to their obsessions. Here, the representation of the *Garuda* figure with scroll petals as soldiers in Maratha style *dhoti* and turban, succeeded by a lion-headed warrior with similar clothing appears on this strut. Two parrots are shown above the shoulders of this warrior out of which one is shown with a lotus bud in its beak.

With reference to the parrots symbolising the British, another equally important and correlated event in the form of an army camp under the leadership of a brave son of the soil can be observed. The history of the first war of Indian independence reveals that one of the closest confederate of the Rani of Jhansi who fought against the British in close association with the Rani was the famous Tatya Tope. Thus it can be assumed that he has been depicted as the lion-headed warrior in this carving to keep the identity of the artist a closely guarded secret, to leave him untouched from the prevailing political scenario in the aftermath of the war of 1857.

In the Indian context, the bravest among the braves is termed as *Narasimha* or *Narakeshari*. So the carver has symbolically represented him as a lion-headed man for easy identification by the Indian viewers. The positioning of the parrots on both his shoulders with a lotus bud in the beak of one of the parrots is intelligently carved just to identify the parrots as the British. The lotus bud in the beak of one of the parrots symbolically shows the success of the British in acquiring sufficient political power and territory.

On the strut at the left side of the seventh pillar, the artist has continued the symbolic depictions of the incidents of the war of 1857. Here, at the bottom, the artist has carved the figure of a *Gajashardula* succeeded by Maratha soldiers in offensive spirit as petals arising out of the lotus scroll. Here, the parrots are shown in two postures, one as pecking at the knee of a Maratha soldier and the second as pecking the stem of the lotus scroll. The lady-warrior at the top of this strut is shown busy in a combat with a naked sword. The figure of a parrot squatting on the chest of a lady-warrior is carved at the top right hand corner of this strut. Even some of the women-warriors are shown underneath the parrots. One remarkable figure is the pecking of the turban of a *tutari* or clarinet player by a parrot. The bottom right side of the seventh strut bears a nice figure of a *Gajashardula* succeeded by a parrot, which is in a posture of holding the *Gajashardula* by its tail. One of the borders of this strut is decorated with the figures of *Garuda* and Hanumana and the top middle part bears the figure of a goddess sitting on the back of a lion. She is shown in an aggressive posture carrying a sword and a shield in two of her four hands. Of her two other hands, one hand appears to be busy pulling one of the ears of the lion in order to wake it up and the other hand appears non-existent. The Hanumana figure is carved holding a club in the right hand.

On the front, left and right sides of the strut on the sixth pillar, we find depictions of figures with similar symbolic meanings narrated in the preceding paragraphs regarding *Gajavyala*, parrots and the goddess. The complete underlying meaning of the group of figures in different postures on the seventh strut can be identified as Maratha soldiers in action at the camp of Tatya Tope. The parrots representing the British soldiers are shown in action to secure political power from the natives through a war. The figure of the Hanumana beside the goddess is symbolic representation of both the heroes of 1857, the figure of the lady-warrior and that of the parrot squatting on her chest can be identified with the power equation of the Marathas vis-a-vis the British at the conclusion of the war.

On the front portion of the strut on the eighth pillar, the figurine of a *Garuda* is depicted at the bottom succeeded by a king and lotus scroll stems on both the sides which are tied with ropes and held in position by the beaks of parrots depicted on either side. At the top is the figure of a goddess surrounded by four parrots.

On the lower part of the strut, a parrot sitting on the lap of the king surrounded by other parrots keeping a close watch is depicted whereas some other parrots are carved in the posture of holding the rope in position from both the sides. At the top, the figures of two parrots are carved on the sides of the queen in a posture of keeping a close watch on the queen. All these parrots with their identification as British soldiers if read in correlation to the history of the period of the first war of independence may reveal some interesting vistas of Indian history.

Appointment of Political Agents in different courts of the native rulers succeeded the outcome of the first war of freedom. The stem of the lotus scroll signifying the progress of native states had been tied with nine knots from the sides and held in position by the beaks of parrots from sides which is symbolic of how the British had succeeded in arresting the progress of Indian native states.

On the left strut of the same pillar, the figure of *Gajashardula* and that of a Maratha soldier in a relaxing posture are carved which is succeeded by a parrot squatting on the neck of the *Gajavyala.* A second parrot is positioned at the head of the *Gajavyala* apparently in a posture of being fed from the right hand of a half-clad Maratha soldier. This portrayal clearly indicates how the parrots had managed to outmaneuver the *Gajashardula* in the race to acquiring political power. The underlying significance of this symbolic portrayal reveals how the native states were brought under the control of the British. The half-clad figure at the top indicates the condition of the natives while the picture in its totality signifies the pathetic condition of the Marathas who are either resting or feeding the British soldiers although they were themselves economically not very well off.

The figure of a Maratha soldier with sword and shield can be noticed at the rear of the *Gajashardula* depicted on the strut at the right side of the same pillar. The upper part of the *Gajashardula* is depicted with a crane sitting on its head and holding the toe of the Maratha king who figures at the top. Once again, the parrots are figured here holding the knots by their beaks.

If these symbols were properly interpreted, they would mean the unfortunate defeat of the Maratha soldiers marked by the rear part of the *Gajashardula* and the positioning of the Maratha soldier apparently with crossed-legs. The figure of the *Gajashardula* with a crane over its head marks the famous British policy of "honey-tongued with a heart of the gull". The posture of the crane attempting to catch hold of the king depicted above indicates the application of this policy.

At the front part of the eighth pillar, as well as on the left and right parts, two important outcomes of the war of 1857 have been clearly depicted, namely the acceptance of British Agents in the courts of native rulers and the British policy towards Indian princely states under their dominion.

The figures on the strut of the ninth pillar are mere representation of those on the strut of the eighth pillar with minor variations. At the front part of this pillar, a change in the pattern of designing the parrot sitting on the lap of the king can be noticed. This parrot appears to be eyeing the neck of the king with soldiers carved above. On the left, a slight change from the figures of the eighth pillar in designing the parrot can be noticed. In the panel on the eighth pillar, the figure of a parrot resting on the shoulders of a Maratha soldier is not noticed whereas the parrots at the top are not shown as busily pecking as is the case with the parrots depicted at the left of the eighth pillar.

At the right side of the strut of eighth pillar, a Maratha soldier apparently in a suicidal position with an inverted weapon can be noticed. At the top, replacement of a crane by parrots can be seen. The crane depicted at the top right side of the strut on the eighth pillar is apparently in a position of catching hold of the foot of the Maratha king by its claws. In addition to these figures, other parrots can be seen holding the knot of the lotus scroll in their beaks.

To sum up the observations of the depictions on the struts on the eighth and ninth pillars it may be said that these depictions convey the pathetic consequences of the first war of Indian independence that the Marathas had to experience as the ultimate outcome. The apparent mood of the parrot sitting on the lap of the king signifies a comfortable position or higher status gained by the British in those days. This clearly indicates the changing political scenario and equations persistently occurring during that period. Moreover, the mood of the parrot sitting on the lap of the king, in the carvings on the front of the ninth pillar is different from that of the eighth pillar. At the eighth pillar, the parrot sitting on the lap of the king appears to be conspiring with the others whereas the parrot on the ninth pillar appears to be eyeing the king and the soldiers depicted above.

The underlying message conveyed by these figures indicates that the British were not satisfied with the Residential status only. Their ambition was to hold the native sovereigns by their neck and oust them.

At the front part of the tenth pillar, the figure of a *Garuda* is carved at the lowest point of the panel succeeded by a Maratha soldier holding a sword in both his hands and standing in a *tribhanga* style (a resting position). The lotus scrolls depicted above him are held at the joints from both sides by the parrots in their beaks. At the top, the figure of a king holding a sword and a shield in both his hands while sitting on a lotus throne is carved. Two lion-heads positioned on either sides of the king appear to convey that the king was under continuous surveillance.

On the left strut of the tenth pillar, the depiction of the figure of a *Gajavyala*, whose hind position is occupied by a Maratha king with figures of monkey under his throne succeeded by a lion and a British dignitary (on a chair) can be observed. The depiction of the lion whispering into the ear of the British sitting on a chair implies the pitiable state of titular native rulers. Here, the *Gajavyala* is shown with a parrot sitting on its trunk and is being patted by a roaring lion at the top. Here in this position, the figure of a lion is used to convey the protection and patronage extended by the British to their kinship depicted as parrots.

However, the figure of the lion in the middle, is used to convey a diagonally opposite meaning. Here, this lion in the middle of the strut depicted as whispering into the left ear of one of the British implies the whispering of some of the titular local rulers apparently engaged in an act of betrayal against their brothers-in-arms in collusion with the British.

The hind portion of the *Vyala* at the left strut of the tenth panel is occupied by a British on a chair, with a lion whispering into his left ear from the side, make it easy to conclude that this scene is the proof of some of the natives being busy in collusion against their brothers-in-arms. The half-clad Maratha gentry on the throne with monkeys underneath is indicative of the fact that these figures represent the futile continuity of the efforts of the native rulers to strengthen their seats. In other words, it may be interpreted that although the natives were defeated but they had not lost forever. Their efforts to gain their former status were alive though such efforts were not concrete yet these can be termed as *markatachesta* meaning thereby the persistent efforts of a monkey to gain its objective.

On the top left side of the tenth and eleventh pillars, we find that, one lion is depicted as patting a parrot by its right forepaw whereas protecting another parrot by its right rear-paw. The patting of parrots by one lion and whispering of another lion are the two positions that are attributed to the lions by the artist on this panel. Both the lions are used with opposite characteristics. While on one hand, the top lion depicts the British, on the other, the lion at the middle portrays the native principality. The functioning of the native kingdoms in the 19th century India as observed and experienced by the artists are appropriately and vividly depicted in these panels as silent proofs.

At the right strut of this panel, the figure of a *Gajavyala* is carved. This figure is succeeded by the figure of a British military officer who is holding a gun in his hands in an ambushing position. The figure of a lion is depicted at his side, whose left rear-paw and right fore paw are placed on the right feet and on the left knee of the British dignitary respectively. The lion is apparently in a position of whispering into the right ear of the dignitary. The lion is carved with the figure of another British soldier aiming at him with his gun from the rear. The panel continues with the depiction of the figure of a *Gajavyala* succeeded by a lion being carved at the head of the *Gajavyala*. The figure of the top lion appears to be patting a parrot by its right fore-paw.

The figures on the tenth pillar are clearer than those on the preceding pillars. This could help in deciphering the significance and meanings of the symbolic carvings on the rest of the pillars. In other words, the tenth pillar holds the key to the opening up of a new vista in the history of the people's movement for the freedom of the nation. The picture of a total defeat suffered by the native sovereigns and the evidence of subsequent British policy towards them, vis-a-vis the status of the Residents and Agents depicted as parrots patronised by the top lion or the king are the significant carvings on this strut. The leisurely mood of Marathas is symbolically portrayed through the depiction of a Maratha soldier in a resting position. The subordinate and subservient status to which the former native sovereigns were subjected to, is aptly reflected through that of a king at the top being guarded by lions from both the sides. The knot of the lotus stem being held by the parrots in their beaks implies the close supervision of the progress of the native states by the British.

The carvings on the left strut of the tenth pillar show the subversive activities of the natives befittingly represented through the figures of monkeys carved under the throne. The portrayal and placement of these monkeys would also imply the futile conspiracies of the natives against the British. The depiction of a lion whispering into the left ear of one of the British sitting on a chair in the middle of the *Gajavyala* figure appears on the strut. It is indicative of the defeat and success of some natives against the British though the British had established themselves in power. The hind position and the successive upper position of the *Gajavyala* reveals the pitiable status of the then native rulers. The hind position followed by the British by establishing themselves on the chair and the upper position succeeded by the top lion are carved to show its secondary status.

The depictions on the struts of the tenth pillar conjointly hint at the famous British policy of divide and rule. The lion whispering into the ear of a British dignitary not only implies the acceptance of British rule by the native sovereigns but also indicates the instinctive whispering of such sovereigns into the ears of the British against the rulers of their neighbouring states, although it is constantly being targeted from behind as shown by the portrayal of a British soldier aiming at the lion from below. Rest of the panel continues to have the figure of a large *Gajavyalas*.

The carvings on the tenth pillar reveal the complete and the total defeat of the native sovereigns. This holds the key to the meaning of the other pillars. The policy pursued by the British to govern the native states is clearly illustrated by the position and postures of the parrots, lions and the soldiers. Here, we find the confirmatory evidences of the completely routed native forces and the higher status gained by the Residents and Agents depicted as parrots being patronised by the true Regent represented by the figure of the lion at the top.

The carvings on the strut of the eleventh pillar are a mere extension of those on the tenth pillar barring two exceptions only. At the left strut of the eleventh pillar the depiction of a half-clad figure of a Maratha gentry seated in a lotus posture (*Padmasana*) as depressed and worried is more or less at the same position of the British soldiers depicted on the preceding pillar.

Through the carvings on the left and the right struts of the eleventh pillar, the artist has successfully pointed out the firm foothold gained by the British in India and the subsequent degradation of native rulers to mere secondary status. The astonishing mood of the Marathas has been intentionally carved by the artist to show their surprise over the success of their rivals, i.e. the British. This clearly shows the position of the trading community (the British in India), who were in the process of slowly but steadily acquiring the driving seat of the administration or the government of this nation, which is a surprising matter for the Indian natives as it was the Vaishyas acquiring the throne of the Kshatriyas in clear contrast to the traditional sentiments and ethics of Indians. The artists had achieved the zenith of expression by portraying sentiments of their land and the people by carving the expression of surprise on the faces of their rulers. And here we are compelled to acknowledge the super-intelligence of the artists in their selection of symbols for their cause.

On the twelfth pillar, the figure of Hanumana holding a club in his left hand is prominently portrayed. His right hand is apparently engaged in lifting his right foot with due care and caution so that the lady beneath is not trampled by the weight of his foot. An iron chain has been apparently fastened around his waist. A parrot with a searching glance is depicted at the side. The identity of Hanumana depicted on this pillar has been deciphered as the firm personality of Tatya Tope.

The adventures of Tatya Tope were the talk of the towns of Gujarat in 1857. He remained in the memory of the people even after 1859. The woodcarver has made sincere efforts to depict such a hero through the symbolic depiction of the figure of Hanumana. Here, he has been portrayed not merely as a close compatriot of famous queen of Jhansi but also as one of her closest friend, philosopher and guide who had been guarding and guiding her. In this panel, she has been depicted as a corpse yet the master soldier, Tatya Tope has been shown as lifting his right leg so as to save her from being trampled. Through the fastening of a chain around his waist and by the depictions of watchful parrots at the side, the carver has tried to convey that the hero was still considered a fugitive who had to be kept under close surveillance by the British.

The use of such a religious symbol as Lord Hanumana, has been made to signify the unshakable devotion and unflinching loyalty of Tatya Tope, which is further supported by the carvings on the other pillars of this complex.

On the iconographic interpretation of the woodcarvings, the thoughts of Clifford Geertz appear to be most appropriate. According to him, "What we call our data are really our own construction of other people's constructions of what they and their compatriots are up to".

A danger exists in mistaking the lines drawn with ink and words in the carved images and interpreting them in their proper perspectives to be appreciated by the world inhabited by the viewers, where images and symbols overlap in ways that cannot be fully interpreted, but still references to the elements can be mentioned in the conversation of it. However, it permits us to understand the correlation and connection between some, of what appear to be a hitherto hidden phenomenon in the woodcarving. It is like trying to read faded, full of ellipses, incoherent, suspicious, emended and tendentious carvings. However, it may not be in a conventionalised style of some sound but in transient examples of shaped behaviours.

Finally, without drawing definite conclusion, I place facts and figures along with my interpretation of the subject before the viewers and readers, and leave them to judge the identification of these carvings themselves.